Windows 8 Apps Revealed

Using XAML and C#

Adam Freeman

Apress®

Apress Media

Windows 8 Apps Revealed: Using XAML and C#

ISBN-13 (pbk): 978-1-4302-5034-0

ISBN-13 (electronic): 978-1-4302-5035-7

President and Publisher of Apress: Paul Manning
Lead Editor: Ewan Buckingham
Technical Reviewer: Fabio Claudio Ferracchiati
Apress Editorial Board: Steve Anglin, Ewan Buckingham, Gary Cornell, Louise Corrigan, Morgan Ertel, Jonathan Gennick, Jonathan Hassell, Robert Hutchinson, Michelle Lowman, James Markham, Matthew Moodie, Jeff Olson, Jeffrey Pepper, Douglas Pundick, Ben Renow-Clarke, Dominic Shakeshaft, Gwenan Spearing, Matt Wade, Tom Welsh
Coordinating Editor: Mark Powers
Copy Editor: Kim Wimpsett
Compositor: SPi Global
Indexer: SPi Global
Artist: SPi Global
Cover Designer: Anna Ishchenko

Distributed to the book trade worldwide by Springer Science+Business Media New York, 233 Spring Street, 6th Floor, New York, NY 10013. Phone 1-800-SPRINGER, fax (201) 348-4505, e-mail orders-ny@springer-sbm.com, or visit www.springeronline.com.

For information on translations, please e-mail rights@apress.com, or visit www.apress.com.

Apress and friends of ED books may be purchased in bulk for academic, corporate, or promotional use. Ebook versions and licenses are also available for most titles. For more information, reference our Special Bulk Sales–eBook Licensing web page at www.apress.com/bulk-sales.

Any source code or other supplementary materials referenced by the author in this text is available to readers at www.apress.com/9781430250340. For detailed information about how to locate your book's source code, go to www.apress.com/source-code

Dedicated to my lovely wife, Jacqui Griffyth.
—Adam Freeman

Contents at a Glance

Contents

About the Author

Adam Freeman is an experienced IT professional who has held senior positions in a range of companies, most recently serving as chief technology officer and chief operating officer of a global bank. Now retired, he spends his time writing and running.

His other upcoming publications include:

Pro Windows 8 Development in HTML5 and JavaScript

Pro ASP.NET MVC 4

His other publications include:

The Definitive Guide to HTML5	*Pro ASP.NET 4 in C# 2010 4th Edition*
Applied ASP.NET 4 in Context	*Pro ASP.NET 4 in VB 2010 3rd Edition*
Pro ASP.NET MVC 3 Framework 3rd Edition	*Pro LINQ*
Pro jQuery	*Pro .NET 4 Parallel Programming in C#*
Introducing Visual C# 2010	*Visual C# 2010 Recipes*

About the Technical Reviewer

Fabio Claudio Ferracchiati is a senior consultant and a senior analyst/developer using Microsoft technologies. He works for Brain Force (www.brainforce.com) in its Italian branch (www.brainforce.it). He is a Microsoft Certified Solution Developer for .NET, a Microsoft Certified Application Developer for .NET, a Microsoft Certified Professional, and a prolific author and technical reviewer. Over the past ten years, he's written articles for Italian and international magazines and coauthored more than ten books on a variety of computer topics.

Acknowledgments

I would like to thank everyone at Apress for working so hard to bring this book to print. In particular, I would like to thank Mark Powers for keeping me on track and Ewan Buckingham for commissioning and editing this book. I would also like to thank my technical reviewer, Fabio, whose efforts made this book far better than it would have been otherwise.

CHAPTER 1

■ ■ ■

Getting Started

Windows Store apps are an important addition to Microsoft Windows 8, providing the cornerstone for a single, consistent programming and interaction model across desktops, tablets, and smartphones. The app user experience is very different from previous generations of Windows applications: Windows Store apps are full-screen and favor a style that is simple, direct, and free from distractions.

Windows Store apps represent a complete departure from previous versions of Windows. There are entirely new APIs, new interaction controls, and a very different approach to managing the life cycle of applications.

Windows Store apps can be developed using a range of languages, including JavaScript, Visual Basic, C++, and, the topic of this book, C#. Windows 8 builds on the familiar to let developers use their existing C# and XAML experience to build rich apps and integrate into the wider Windows platform. This book gives you an essential jump start into the world of Windows Store apps; by the end, you will understand how to use the controls and features that define the core Windows Store app experience.

■ **Note** Microsoft uses the term *Windows Store App*, which I find awkward, and I can't bring myself to use it throughout this book. Instead, I'll refer to *Windows apps* and, often, just plain *apps*. I'll leave you to mentally insert the official Microsoft names as you see fit.

About This Book

This book is for experienced C# developers who want to get a head start creating apps for Windows 8. I explain the concepts and techniques you need to get up to speed quickly and to boost your app development techniques and knowledge

What Do You Need to Know Before You Read This Book?

You need to have a good understanding of C# and, ideally, of XAML. If you have worked on WPF or Silverlight projects, then you will have enough XAML knowledge to build Windows apps. Don't worry if you haven't worked with XAML before; you can pick it up as you go, and I give you a very brief overview later in this chapter to get you started. I'll be calling out the major XAML concepts as I use them.

1

What Software Do You Need for This Book?

You need two things for Windows app development: a PC running Windows 8 and Visual Studio 2012. You'll need to buy a copy of Windows 8 if you get serious about Windows app development, but if you are just curious, then you can get a 90-day trial from Microsoft from http://msdn.microsoft.com/en-us/evalcenter. You'll find what you need by clicking the Release link in the Windows and Platform Development section.

You are required to create a Microsoft account to get the evaluation, but you'll need one of those anyway to get set up as a developer. Microsoft accounts are free to create, and there are instructions to follow if you don't already have one.

■ **Tip**   You can run Windows 8 in a virtual machine, but for the best results I recommend installing the operating system directly onto a PC.

Visual Studio 2012 is Microsoft's development environment. The good news is that Microsoft makes a basic version of Visual Studio available for free, and that's the version I'll be using in this book. It has the catchy name of *Visual Studio 2012 Express for Windows 8*, and you can download the installer from www.microsoft.com/visualstudio/11/en-us/products/express. Several flavors are available, each of which can be used to develop a specific kind of application. For app development, you will need *Visual Studio Express 2012 for Windows 8*. The names of the different flavors are confusingly similar, so be sure to download the right one.

The free version doesn't have all of the testing and integration features that some of the paid-for versions of Visual Studio contain, but you don't need those to create Windows apps. In all other respects, the free version of Visual Studio is fully featured and does everything you will need.

■ **Tip**   Don't worry if you have a paid-for version of Visual Studio 2012. You won't need all of the features in your edition, but all of the instructions and examples in this book will work without any problems or modification.

Install Visual Studio as you would any other app. Although the software is free, you will need to activate it, which requires the Microsoft account you created earlier. After you have gone through the process, you'll end up with a code that you can use to activate Visual Studio. You will also need a developer license, which is free as well. When you first start Visual Studio 2012, you will be prompted to obtain a license; it takes only a second, and, once again, it requires the Microsoft account you created earlier.

■ **Note**   Although Visual Studio and the Microsoft account are free, you will have to pay if you want to publish apps to the Windows Store. Microsoft currently charges $49 per year for individuals and $99 per year for companies, but you may be entitled to free publishing if you subscribe to Microsoft packages such as MSDN.

What Is the Structure of This Book?

I focus on the key techniques and features that make a Windows app. You already know how to write C#, and I am not going to waste your time teaching you what you already know. This book is about translating your C# and XAML development experience into the Windows app world, and that means focusing on what makes a Windows app different and special.

I have taken a relaxed approach to mixing topics. Aside from the main theme in each chapter, you'll find some essential context to explain why features are important and why you should implement them. By the end of this book, you will understand how to build a Windows app that integrates properly into Windows 8 and presents a user experience that is consistent with apps written using other languages, such as C++ or JavaScript.

This is a primer to get you started on app development for Windows 8. It isn't a comprehensive tutorial; as a consequence, I have focused on those topics that are the major building blocks for an app. There is a lot of information that I just couldn't fit into such a slim volume. If you do want more comprehensive coverage of Windows app development, then Apress has published Jesse Liberty's *Pro Windows 8 Development with XAML and C#*. In addition, Apress will publish my *Pro Windows 8 Development with HTML5 and JavaScript book* if you want to use more web-oriented technologies to build your apps.

The following sections summarize the chapters in this book.

Chapter 1: Getting Started

This chapter. Aside from introducing this book, I show you how to create the Visual Studio project for the example app that I use throughout this book. I give you a brief overview of XAML, take you on a tour of the important files in an app development project, show you how to run your apps in the Visual Studio simulator, and explain how to use the debugger.

Chapter 2: Data, Bindings, and Pages

Data is at the heart of any Windows app, and in this chapter I show you how to define a view model and how to use data bindings to bring that data into your app layouts. These techniques are essential to building apps that are easy to extend, easy to test, and easy to maintain. Along the way, I'll show you how to use *pages* to break your app into manageable chunks of XAML and C# code.

Chapter 3: AppBars, Flyouts, and NavBars

Some user interface controls are common to all Windows apps, regardless of which language is used to create them. In this chapter, I show you how to create and configure AppBars, Flyouts, and NavBars, which are the most important of these common controls; together they form the backbone of your interaction with the user.

Chapter 4: Layouts and Tiles

The functionality of a Windows app extends to the Windows 8 Start menu, which offers a number of ways to present the user with additional information. In this chapter, I show you how to create and update dynamic Start tiles and how to apply *badges* to those tiles.

I also show you how to deal with the *snapped* and *filled* layouts, which allow a Windows 8 user to use two Windows apps side by side. You can adapt to these layouts using just C# code or a mix of code and XAML. I show you both approaches.

Chapter 5: App Life Cycle and Contracts

Windows applies a very specific life-cycle model to apps. In this chapter, I explain how the model works, show you how to receive and respond to the most life-cycle events, and explain how to manage the transitions between a *suspended* and *running* app. I demonstrate how to create and manage asynchronous tasks and how to bring them under control when your app is suspended. Finally, I show you how to support *contracts*, which allow your app to seamlessly integrate into the wider Windows 8 experience.

More About the Example Windows App

The example app for this book is a simple grocery list manager called *GrocerApp*. As an app in its own right, GrocerApp is pretty dull, but it is a perfect platform to demonstrate the most important app features. In Figure 1-1, you can see how the app will look by the end of this book.

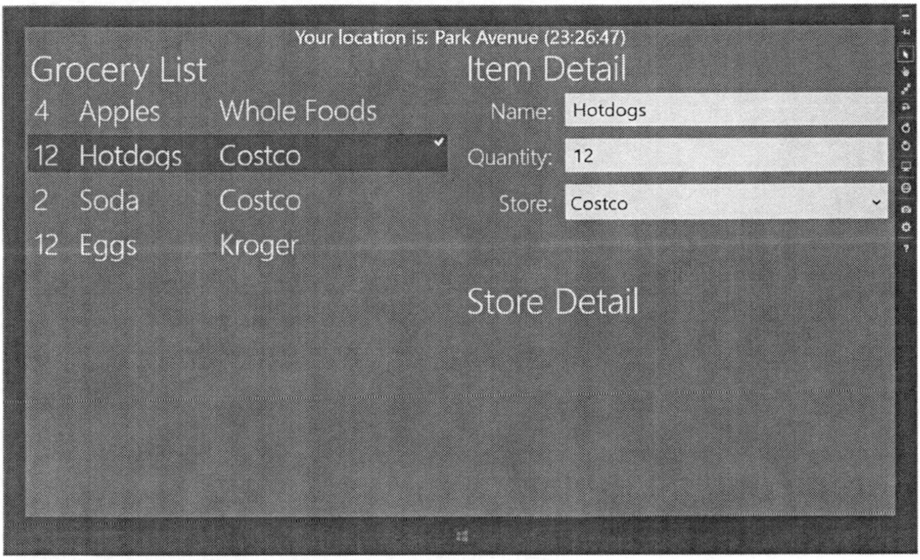

Figure 1-1. *The example app*

This is a book about programming and not design. GrocerApp is not a pretty app, and I don't even implement all of its features. It is a vehicle for demonstrating coding techniques, pure and simple.

Is There a Lot of Code in This Book?

Yes. In fact, there is so much code that I couldn't fit it all in without some editing. So, when I introduce a new topic or make a lot of changes, I'll show you a complete C# or XAML file. When I make small changes or want to emphasize a few critical lines of code or markup, I'll show you a code fragment and highlight the important changes. You can see what this looks like in Listing 1-1, which is taken from Chapter 5.

Listing 1-1. A Code Fragment

```
...
protected override void OnNavigatedTo(NavigationEventArgs e) {
    viewModel = (ViewModel)e.Parameter;

    ItemDetailFrame.Navigate(typeof(NoItemSelected));
    viewModel.PropertyChanged += (sender, args) => {
        if (args.PropertyName == "SelectedItemIndex") {
            groceryList.SelectedIndex = viewModel.SelectedItemIndex;
            if (viewModel.SelectedItemIndex == -1) {
                ItemDetailFrame.Navigate(typeof(NoItemSelected));
                AppBarDoneButton.IsEnabled = false;
```

5

```
        } else {
            ItemDetailFrame.Navigate(typeof(ItemDetail), viewModel);
            AppBarDoneButton.IsEnabled = true;
        }
    }
};
}
...
```

These fragments make it easier for me to pack more code into this slim book, but they make following along with the examples in Visual Studio more difficult. If you do want to follow the examples, then the best way is to download the source code for this book from Apress.com. The code is available for free and includes a complete Visual Studio project for every chapter in the book.

Getting Up and Running

In this section, I'll create the project for the example app and show you each of the project elements that Visual Studio generates. I'll break this process down step-by-step so that you can follow along. If you prefer, you can download the ready-made project from Apress.com.

Creating the Project

To create the example project, start Visual Studio and select File ➤ New Project. In the New Project dialog, select Visual C# from the Templates section on the left of the screen, and select Blank App from the available project templates, as shown in Figure 1-2.

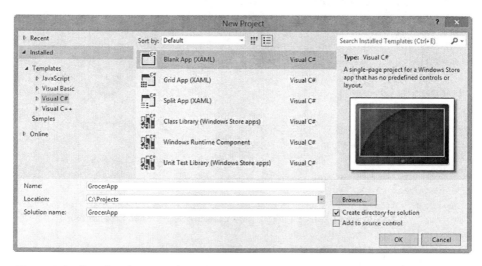

Figure 1-2. Creating the example project

Set the name of the project to GrocerApp, and click the OK button to create the project. Visual Studio will create and populate the project with some initial files.

■ **Tip** Visual Studio includes some basic templates for C# Windows apps. I don't like them, and I think they strike an odd balance between XAML and C# code. For this reason, I will be working with the Blank App template, which creates a project with the bare essentials for app development.

Figure 1-3 shows the contents of the new project as displayed by the Visual Studio Solution Explorer. In the sections that follow, I'll describe the most important files in the project.

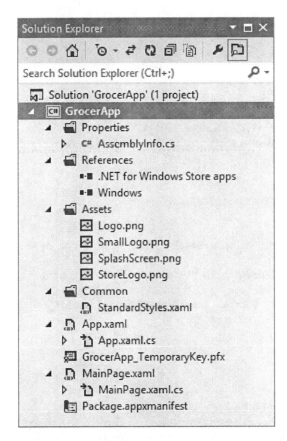

Figure 1-3. The contents of a Visual Studio project created using the Blank App template

> ■ **Tip** Don't worry if the purpose or content of these files isn't immediately obvious. I'll explain everything you need to know as I build the example app. At this stage, I just want you to get a feel for how a Visual Studio app project fits together and what the important files are.

Windows apps use a slimmed-down version of the .NET Framework library. You can see which namespaces are available by double-clicking the .Net for Windows Store apps item in the References section of the Solution Explorer.

Exploring the App.xaml File

The App.xaml file and its code-behind file, App.xaml.cs, are used to start the Windows app. The main use for the XAML file is to associate StandardStyles.xaml from the Common folder with the app, as shown in Listing 1-2.

Listing 1-2. The App.xaml File

```
<Application
    x:Class="GrocerApp.App"
    xmlns="http://schemas.microsoft.com/winfx/2006/xaml/presentation"
    xmlns:x="http://schemas.microsoft.com/winfx/2006/xaml"
    xmlns:local="using:GrocerApp">

    <Application.Resources>
        <ResourceDictionary>
            <ResourceDictionary.MergedDictionaries>

                <!--
                    Styles that define common aspects of the platform look
                        and feel
                    Required by Visual Studio project and item templates
                -->
                <ResourceDictionary Source="Common/StandardStyles.xaml"/>
            </ResourceDictionary.MergedDictionaries>

        </ResourceDictionary>
    </Application.Resources>
</Application>
```

I'll discuss the StandardStyles.xaml file shortly, and, later in this chapter, I'll update App.xaml to reference my own resource dictionary. The code-behind file is much more interesting and is shown in Listing 1-3. (For brevity, I have removed some of the comments that Visual Studio adds to this file.)

Listing 1-3. The App.xaml.cs File

```
using System;
using System.Collections.Generic;
using System.IO;
using System.Linq;
using Windows.ApplicationModel;
using Windows.ApplicationModel.Activation;
using Windows.Foundation;
using Windows.Foundation.Collections;
using Windows.UI.Xaml;
using Windows.UI.Xaml.Controls;
using Windows.UI.Xaml.Controls.Primitives;
using Windows.UI.Xaml.Data;
using Windows.UI.Xaml.Input;
using Windows.UI.Xaml.Media;
using Windows.UI.Xaml.Navigation;

namespace GrocerApp {

    sealed partial class App : Application {

        public App() {
            this.InitializeComponent();
            this.Suspending += OnSuspending;
        }

        protected override void OnLaunched(LaunchActivatedEventArgs args) {
            Frame rootFrame = Window.Current.Content as Frame;

            if (rootFrame == null) {
                // Create a Frame to act as the navigation context
                // and navigate to the first page
                rootFrame = new Frame();
                if (args.PreviousExecutionState ==
                    ApplicationExecutionState.Terminated) {
                    //TODO: Load state from previously suspended application
                }

                // Place the frame in the current Window
                Window.Current.Content = rootFrame;
            }
```

```
        if (rootFrame.Content == null) {

            if (!rootFrame.Navigate(typeof(MainPage), args.Arguments)) {
                throw new Exception("Failed to create initial page");
            }
        }
        // Ensure the current window is active
        Window.Current.Activate();
    }

    private void OnSuspending(object sender, SuspendingEventArgs e) {
        var deferral = e.SuspendingOperation.GetDeferral();
        //TODO: Save application state and stop any background activity
        deferral.Complete();
    }
  }
}
```

Windows apps have a very specific life-cycle model, which is expressed through the App.xaml.cs file. It is essential to understand and embrace this model, which I explain in Chapter 5. For the moment, you need to know only that the OnLaunched method is called when the app is started and that a new instance of the MainPage class is loaded and used as the main interface for the app.

■ **Tip**   For brevity, I have removed most of the comments from these files and removed the namespace references that are not used by the code in the class.

Exploring the MainPage.xaml File

Pages are the basic building blocks for a Windows app. When you create a project using the Blank App template, Visual Studio creates a blank page, which it names MainPage. xaml. Listing 1-4 shows the content of the MainPage.xaml file, which contains just enough XAML to display . . . well, a blank page.

Listing 1-4. The Contents of the MainPage.xaml File

```
<Page
    x:Class="GrocerApp.MainPage"
    xmlns="http://schemas.microsoft.com/winfx/2006/xaml/presentation"
    xmlns:x="http://schemas.microsoft.com/winfx/2006/xaml"
    xmlns:local="using:GrocerApp"
    xmlns:d="http://schemas.microsoft.com/expression/blend/2008"
    xmlns:mc="http://schemas.openxmlformats.org/markup-compatibility/2006"
    mc:Ignorable="d">
```

```
<Grid Background="{StaticResource ApplicationPageBackgroundThemeBrush}">

</Grid>
</Page>
```

If you have used XAML before, you will recognize the Grid control. Windows app UI controls work in generally the same way as those from WPF or Silverlight, but there are fewer of them, and some of the advanced layout and data binding features are not available. I'll create a more useful Page layout in Chapter 2 when I start to build the example project. The code-behind file for MainPage.xaml will also be familiar if you have XAML experience, as shown in Listing 1-5.

■ **Tip** Don't worry about the XAML and code-behind files for the moment; I provide a quick overview later in this chapter.

Listing 1-5. The Contents of the MainPage.xaml.cs File

```csharp
using System;
using System.Collections.Generic;
using System.IO;
using System.Linq;
using Windows.Foundation;
using Windows.Foundation.Collections;
using Windows.UI.Xaml;
using Windows.UI.Xaml.Controls;
using Windows.UI.Xaml.Controls.Primitives;
using Windows.UI.Xaml.Data;
using Windows.UI.Xaml.Input;
using Windows.UI.Xaml.Media;
using Windows.UI.Xaml.Navigation;

namespace GrocerApp {
    public sealed partial class MainPage : Page {
        public MainPage() {
            this.InitializeComponent();
        }

        protected override void OnNavigatedTo(NavigationEventArgs e) {
        }
    }
}
```

Exploring the StandardStyles.xaml File

The Common folder contains files that are used by Visual Studio project templates. The only file in this folder when the Blank App template is used is StandardStyles.xaml, which is the resource dictionary file referred to in the App.xaml file (as shown in Listing 1-2). The StandardStyles.xaml file contains some the styles and templates that make it easier to create an app that has an appearance that is consistent with the broader Windows app look and feel. I am not going to list the complete file because it contains a lot of content, but Listing 1-6 shows an example of a text-related style.

Listing 1-6. A Style from the StandardStyles.xaml File

```
...
<Style x:Key="HeaderTextStyle" TargetType="TextBlock"
        BasedOn="{StaticResource BaselineTextStyle}">
    <Setter Property="FontSize" Value="56"/>
    <Setter Property="FontWeight" Value="Light"/>
    <Setter Property="LineHeight" Value="40"/>
    <Setter Property="RenderTransform">
        <Setter.Value>
            <TranslateTransform X="-2" Y="8"/>
        </Setter.Value>
    </Setter>
</Style>
...
```

▒ **Caution**   Don't edit the files in the Common folder. I'll show you how to create and reference a custom resource dictionary in Chapter 2.

Exploring the Package.appxmanifest File

The final file worth mentioning is the *manifest*, called Package.appxmanifest. This is an XML file that provides information about your app to Windows. You can edit this file as raw XML, but Visual Studio provides a nice properties-based editor to use instead. I'll return to this file in later chapters to configure some of the app settings.

An Incredibly Brief XAML Overview

Don't worry if you haven't used XAML before. The learning curve for creating Windows apps will be steeper, but you have the advantage of not expecting features from other XAML application types that are not available in Windows app development.

At its heart, XAML creates user interfaces declaratively, rather than in code. So, if I wanted to add a couple of button controls to my project, I add some markup to my XAML file, as shown in Listing 1-7.

Listing 1-7. Adding Controls to the XAML Document

```
<Page
    x:Class="GrocerApp.MainPage"
    xmlns="http://schemas.microsoft.com/winfx/2006/xaml/presentation"
    xmlns:x="http://schemas.microsoft.com/winfx/2006/xaml"
    xmlns:local="using:GrocerApp"
    xmlns:d="http://schemas.microsoft.com/expression/blend/2008"
    xmlns:mc="http://schemas.openxmlformats.org/markup-compatibility/2006"
    mc:Ignorable="d">

    <Grid Background="{StaticResource ApplicationPageBackgroundThemeBrush}">
        <StackPanel HorizontalAlignment="Center" VerticalAlignment="Center">
            <Button x:Name="FirstButton" HorizontalAlignment="Center"
                    Click="ButtonClick">Click Me!</Button>
            <Button Style="{StaticResource TextButtonStyle}"
                    HorizontalAlignment="Center"
                    Click="ButtonClick">Or Click Me!</Button>
        </StackPanel>
    </Grid>
</Page>
```

The tag name in a XAML element specifies the control that will be added to the layout. I have added one StackPanel and two Button controls to my project. The StackPanel is a simple container that helps add structure to the layout; it positions its child controls in either a horizontal or vertical line (a *stack*). The Button controls are just what you'd expect: a button that emits an event when the user clicks it.

The hierarchical nature of the XML is translated into the hierarchy of UI controls. By placing the Button elements inside the StackPanel, I have specified that the StackPanel is responsible for the layout of the Button elements.

Using the Visual Studio Design Surface

You can do everything in C# in a Windows app project and not use XAML at all. But there some compelling reasons to adopt XAML. The main advantage is that the design support for XAML in Visual Studio is pretty good and will, for the most part, show you the effect of changes to your XAML files in real time. As Figure 1-4 shows, Visual Studio reflected the addition of the StackPanel and Button elements on its XAML design surface. This isn't the same as running the app, but it is a broadly faithful representation, and this feature isn't available for interfaces created in C#. (The buttons are quite small, so I have magnified them in the figure to make them easier to see).

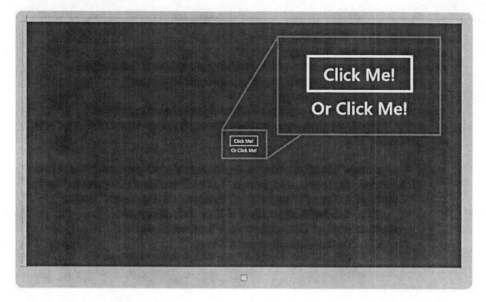

Figure 1-4. *Visual Studio reflecting the contents of a XAML file on its design surface*

Although XAML tends to be verbose, Visual Studio does a lot to make creating and editing it easier; it has some excellent autocomplete features that offer suggestions for tag names, attributes, and values. You can also design an interface by dragging controls from the Toolbox directly onto the design surface and configuring them using the Properties window. If neither of those approaches suits you, there is support for creating the XAML for apps in Blend for Visual Studio, which was installed on your machine as part of the Visual Studio setup. I favor writing the XAML directly in the code editor, but then I am crusty old-school programmer who has never really trusted visual design tools, even though they have become pretty good in recent years. You may not be quite as resistant to change, and you should try the different styles of UI development to see which suits you. For the purposes of this book, I'll show you changes to the XAML directly.

Configuring Controls in XAML

You configure Windows app UI controls by setting attributes on the corresponding XAML element. So, for example, I wanted the StackPanel to center its child controls. To do this, I set values for the HorizontalAlignment and VerticalAlignment attributes, like this:

```
...
<StackPanel HorizontalAlignment="Center" VerticalAlignment="Center">
...
```

Applying Styles

Attributes are also used to apply styles to UI controls. As an example, I applied the TextButtonStyle that is defined by Microsoft in the StandardStyles.xaml file:

```
...
<Button Style="{StaticResource TextButtonStyle}"
HorizontalAlignment="Center"
Click="ButtonClick">Or Click Me!</Button>
...
```

There are different ways to define and reference styles in XAML. I have used StaticResource to specify the style I want, but there are options for getting the style information from all sorts of sources. I am going to keep things simple in this book and stick to the basics wherever possible, focusing on the features that are specific to Windows apps.

Specifying Event Handlers

To specify a handler method for an event, you simply use the element attribute that corresponds to the event you require, like this:

```
...
<Button x:Name="FirstButton" HorizontalAlignment="Center"
    Click="ButtonClick">Click Me!</Button>
...
```

I have specified that the click event (which is triggered when the user clicks the button) will be handled by the ButtonClick method. Visual Studio will offer to create an event handler method for you when you apply an event attribute; I'll show you the other side of this relationship in in the next section.

Configuring Controls in Code

XAML relies on some clever compiler tricks and a C# feature known as *partial* classes. The markup in a XAML file is converted and combined with the code-behind file to create a single .NET class. This can seem a bit odd at first, but it does allow for a nice hybrid model where you can define and configure controls in XAML, the code-behind C# class, or both.

The simplest way of demonstrating this relationship is to show you the implementation of the event handler that I specified for the Button elements in the XAML file.

Listing 1-8 shows the MainPage.xaml.cs file, which is the code-behind file for MainPage.xaml.

Listing 1-8. The MainPage.xaml.cs File

```
using System;
using System.Collections.Generic;
using System.IO;
using System.Linq;
using Windows.Foundation;
using Windows.Foundation.Collections;
using Windows.UI.Xaml;
using Windows.UI.Xaml.Controls;
using Windows.UI.Xaml.Controls.Primitives;
using Windows.UI.Xaml.Data;
using Windows.UI.Xaml.Input;
using Windows.UI.Xaml.Media;
using Windows.UI.Xaml.Navigation;

namespace GrocerApp {
    public sealed partial class MainPage : Page {
        public MainPage() {
            this.InitializeComponent();
        }

        protected override void OnNavigatedTo(NavigationEventArgs e) {
        }

        private void ButtonClick(object sender, RoutedEventArgs e) {
            System.Diagnostics.Debug.WriteLine("Button Clicked: "
                + ((Button)e.OriginalSource).Content);
        }
    }
}
```

I am able to refer to the ButtonClick method without any qualification in the XAML file because the code generated from the XAML file is merged with the C# code in the code-behind file to create a single class. The result is that when one of the Button elements in the app layout is clicked, my C# ButtonClick method is invoked.

■ **Tip** No console is available for Windows apps, so use the static System.Diagnostcs.Debug.WriteLine method if you want to write out messages to help figure out what's going on in your app. These are shown in the Visual Studio Output window, but only if you start your app using Start With Debugging from the Visual Studio Debug menu.

This relationship goes both ways. Notice that some of the elements in the XAML file have an x:Name attribute, like this:

```
...
<Button x:Name="FirstButton" HorizontalAlignment="Center"
    Click="ButtonClick">Click Me!</Button>
...
```

When you specify a value for this attribute, the compiler creates a variable whose value is the UI control that was created from the XAML element. This means you can supplement the XAML configuration of your controls with C# code or change the configuration of elements programmatically. Listing 1-9 shows how I change the configuration of the button whose name is FirstButton in the ButtonClick method defined in the MainPage.xaml.cs code-behind file.

Listing 1-9. Configuring a Control in Code in Response to an Event in the MainPage.xaml.cs File

```
...
private void ButtonClick(object sender, RoutedEventArgs e) {

    FirstButton.Content = "Pressed";
    FirstButton.FontSize = 50;

    System.Diagnostics.Debug.WriteLine("Button Clicked: "
        + ((Button)e.OriginalSource).Content);
}
...
```

I don't have to qualify the control name in any way. In this example, I change the contents of the button and the size of the font. Since these new statements are in the Click event handler function, clicking either button will cause the configuration of the FirstButton to change. That's all you need to know about XAML for the moment. To summarize:

- XAML is converted into code and merged with the contents of the code-behind file to create a single .NET class.

- You can configure UI controls in XAML or in code.

- Using XAML lets you use the Visual Studio design tools, which are pretty good.

XAML may strike you as verbose and hard to read at first, but you will soon get used to it. I find that it is a lot easier to work with XAML than using just C# code, although I admit it took me quite some time with XAML before I decided that was the case.

Running and Debugging a Windows App

Now that I have a very simple Windows app, it is time to focus on how to run and debug it. Visual Studio provides three ways to run an app: on the local machine, on the simulator, or on a remote machine.

The problem with the local machine is that development PCs are rarely configured the way that user devices are. Unless you are targeting your app at people with similar spec platforms, then testing on the local machine doesn't give you a representative view of how your app will behave.

Testing on a remote machine is the best approach, but only if you have a range of machines with different capabilities to test with. I have a cheap Dell Duo laptop that has a touchscreen and some hardware sensors that make it useful for testing, but it can quickly become expensive to build a stable of suitable test machines.

The best compromise is the Visual Studio *simulator*, which provides a faithful representation of the Windows app experience and lets you change the capabilities of the device you are simulating (including changing the screen size), simulate touch events, and generate synthetic geolocation data.

To select the simulator, locate the button on the Visual Studio toolbar that currently says Local Machine, and click the small downward arrow just to the right of it. Select Simulator from the pop-up menu, as shown in Figure 1-5.

Figure 1-5. *Selecting the Visual Studio simulator to test apps*

Running a Windows App in the Simulator

To start the example app, click the toolbar button (which will now say Simulator), or select Start with Debug from the Debug menu. Visual Studio will start the simulator and build and deploy the app, as shown in Figure 1-6.

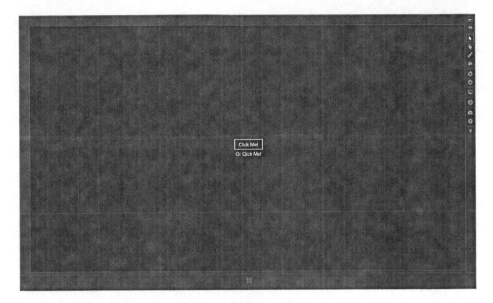

Figure 1-6. Using the Visual Studio simulator

You can use the buttons on the right side of the simulator to change the screen size and orientation, switch between mouse and touch input, and synthesize geolocation data. There isn't much to see because the example app is very simple at the moment.

Click either of the buttons on the app layout to trigger the event handler method and change the configuration of the button. Figure 1-7 shows the result.

Figure 1-7. The result of clicking either of the buttons in the example app

You will also see a message in the Output window, similar to the following:

```
Button Clicked: Pressed
```

The Output window may not be shown by default. You can open it by selecting the Output item from the Debug ➤ Windows menu in Visual Studio.

19

Since the app is running in the debugger, any exceptions will cause the debugger to break, allowing you to step through the code just as you would a regular C# project. You can force the debugger to break by setting breakpoints in the source code; aside from the use of the simulator, running and debugging a Windows app uses the standard Visual Studio facilities.

Summary

In this chapter, I provided an overview of this book and introduced the basics of a Windows app written using XAML and C#. I provided a very basic overview of XAML and showed you how it can be applied to create a simple example app. In the next chapter, I'll start to build the app to add the major structural components, starting with a view model.

CHAPTER 2

■ ■ ■

Data, Binding, and Pages

In this chapter, I show you how to define and use the data that forms the core of a Windows app. To do this, I will be loosely following the *view model* pattern, which allows me to cleanly separate the data from the parts of the app responsible for displaying that data and handling user interactions.

You may already be familiar with view models from design patterns such as Model-View-Controller (MVC) and Model-View-View Controller (MVVC). I am not going to get into the details of these patterns in this book. There is a lot of good information about MVC and MVVC available, starting with Wikipedia, which has some balanced and insightful descriptions.

I find the benefits of using a view model to be enormous and well worth considering for all but the simplest app projects, and I recommend you seriously consider following the same path. I am not a pattern zealot, and I firmly believe in taking the parts of patterns and techniques that solve real problems and adapting them to work in specific projects. To that end, you will find that I take a liberal view of how a view model should be used.

This chapter focuses on the behind-the-scenes plumbing in an app, creating a foundation that I can build to demonstrate different features. I start slowly, defining a simple view model, and demonstrate different techniques for bringing the data from the view model into the app display using data binding. I then show you how you can break down your app into multiple pages and bring those pages into the main layout, changing which pages are used to reflect the state of your app. Table 2-1 provides the summary for this chapter.

Table 2-1. *Chapter Summary*

Problem	Solution	Listing
Create an observable class.	Implement the INotifyPropertyChanged interface.	1
Create an observable collection.	Use the ObservableCollection class.	2
Change the Page loaded when an app starts.	Change the type specified in the OnLaunched method in App.xaml.cs.	3
Set the source for data binding values.	Use the DataContext property.	4

(*continued*)

Table 2-1. (*continued*)

Problem	Solution	Listing
Create reusable styles and templates.	Create a resource dictionary.	5, 6
Bind UI controls to the view model.	Use the Binding keyword.	7
Add another Page to the app layout.	Add a Frame to the main layout and use the Navigate method to specify the Page to display.	8–10
Dynamically insert pages into the app layout.	Use the Frame.Navigate method, optionally passing a context object to the embedded Page.	11–14

Adding a View Model

At the heart of a good Windows app is a *view model*, the use of which lets me keep my app data separate from the way it is presented to the user. View models are an essential foundation for creating apps that are easy to enhance and maintain over time. It can be tempting to treat the data contained in a particular UI control as being authoritative, but you will soon reach a point where figuring out where your data is and how it should be updated is unmanageable.

To begin, I have created a new folder in the Visual Studio project called Data and have created a two new class files. The first defines the GroceryItem class, which represents a single item on the grocery list. You can see the contents of GroceryItem.cs in Listing 2-1.

Listing 2-1. The GroceryItem Class

```
using System.ComponentModel;

namespace GrocerApp.Data {

    public class GroceryItem : INotifyPropertyChanged {
        private string name, store;
        private int quantity;

        public string Name {
            get { return name; }
            set { name = value; NotifyPropertyChanged("Name"); }
        }

        public int Quantity {
            get { return quantity; }
            set { quantity = value; NotifyPropertyChanged("Quantity"); }
        }
```

```
        public string Store {
            get { return store; }
            set { store = value; NotifyPropertyChanged("Store"); }
        }

        public event PropertyChangedEventHandler PropertyChanged;
        private void NotifyPropertyChanged(string propName) {
            if (PropertyChanged != null) {
                PropertyChanged(this, new PropertyChangedEventArgs(propName));
            }
        }
    }
}
```

This class defines properties for the name and quantity of the item to be purchased and which store it should be bought from. The only noteworthy aspect of this class is that it is *observable*. One of the nice features about the Windows App UI controls is that they support data binding, which means they automatically update when the observable data they are displaying is changed.

You implement the System.ComponentModel.INotifyPropertyChanged interface to make classes observable and trigger the PropertyChangedEventHandler specified by the interface when any of the observable properties is modified.

The other class I added in the Data namespace is ViewModel, which is contained in ViewModel.cs. This class contains the user data and the app state, and you can see the definition of the class in Listing 2-2.

Listing 2-2. The ViewModel Class

```
using System.Collections.Generic;
using System.Collections.ObjectModel;
using System.ComponentModel;

namespace GrocerApp.Data {

    public class ViewModel : INotifyPropertyChanged {
        private ObservableCollection<GroceryItem> groceryList;
        private List<string> storeList;
        private int selectedItemIndex;
        private string homeZipCode;

        public ViewModel() {
            groceryList = new ObservableCollection<GroceryItem>();
            storeList = new List<string>();
            selectedItemIndex = -1;
            homeZipCode = "NY 10118";
        }
```

```
        public string HomeZipCode {
            get { return homeZipCode; }
            set { homeZipCode = value; NotifyPropertyChanged("HomeZipCode"); }
        }

        public int SelectedItemIndex {
            get { return selectedItemIndex; }
            set {
                selectedItemIndex = value;
                NotifyPropertyChanged("SelectedItemIndex");
            }
        }

        public ObservableCollection<GroceryItem> GroceryList {
            get {
                return groceryList;
            }
        }

        public List<string> StoreList {
            get {
                return storeList;
            }
        }

        public event PropertyChangedEventHandler PropertyChanged;
        private void NotifyPropertyChanged(string propName) {
            if (PropertyChanged != null) {
                PropertyChanged(this, new PropertyChangedEventArgs(propName));
            }
        }
    }
}
```

The most important part of this simple view model is the collection of
GroceryItem objects that represent the grocery list. I want the list to be observable so
that changes to the list are automatically updated in the app UI. To do this, I use an
ObservableCollection from the System.Collections.ObjectModel namespace. This
class implements the basic features of a collection and emits events when list items are
added, removed, or replaced. The ObservableCollection class doesn't emit an event
when the data values of one of the objects it contains are modified, but by creating an
observable collection of observable GroceryList objects, I make sure that *any* change to
the grocery list will result in an update in the UI.

The ViewModel class implements the INotifyPropertyChanged as well, because
there are two observable properties in the view model. The first, HomeZipCode, is user
data, and I'll use that in Chapter 3 when I demonstrate how to create *flyouts*. The second
observable property, SelectedItemIndex, is part of the app state and keeps track of which
item in the grocery list the user has selected, if any.

This is a very simple view model, and as I mentioned, I take a liberal view of how I structure view models in my projects. That said, it contains all of the ingredients I need to demonstrate how to use data binding to keep my app UI controls automatically updated.

Adding the Main Layout

Now that I have defined the view model, I can start to put together the UI. The first step is to add the main page for the app. I understand why Visual Studio generates a page called `MainPage`, but I want to show you how I tend to structure my projects, so I am going to add a new page to the project.

▨ **Tip**   I won't be using `MainPage.xaml` again, so you can delete it from your project.

I like to work with a lot of project structure, so I have added a new folder to the project called `Pages`. I added a new `Blank Page` called `ListPage.xaml` by right-clicking the `Pages` folder, selecting Add ➤ New Item from the pop-up menu, and selecting the Blank Page template. Visual Studio creates the XAML file and the code-behind file, `ListPage.xaml.cs`.

▨ **Tip**   If you are new to building apps using XAML, then it is important to understand that you wouldn't usually work in the order in which I described the example app. Instead, the XAML approach supports a more iterative style where you declare some controls using XAML, add some code to support them, and perhaps define some styles to reduce duplication in the markup. It is a much more natural process than I have made it appear here, but it is hard to capture the back-and-forth nature of XAML-based development in a book.

I want to make `ListPage.xaml` the page that is loaded when my app is started, which requires an update to `App.xaml.cs`, as shown in Listing 2-3.

Listing 2-3. Updating App.xaml.cs to Use the ListPage

```
using System;
using Windows.ApplicationModel;
using Windows.ApplicationModel.Activation;
using Windows.UI.Xaml;
using Windows.UI.Xaml.Controls;

namespace GrocerApp {

    sealed partial class App : Application {

        public App() {
```

```
            this.InitializeComponent();
            this.Suspendin += OnSuspending;
        }

        protected override void OnLaunched(LaunchActivatedEventArgs args) {
            Frame rootFrame = Window.Current.Content as Frame;


            if (rootFrame == null) {
                rootFrame = new Frame();

                if (args.PreviousExecutionState == ApplicationExecutionState.
                                            Terminated) {
                    //TODO: Load state from previously suspended application
                }

                // Place the frame in the current Window
                Window.Current.Content = rootFrame;
            }

            if (rootFrame.Content == null) {

                if (!rootFrame.Navigate(typeof(Pages.ListPage),
                    args.Arguments)) {
                    throw new Exception("Failed to create initial page");
                }
            }
            // Ensure the current window is active
            Window.Current.Activate();
        }

        private void OnSuspending(object sender, SuspendingEventArgs e) {
            var deferral = e.SuspendingOperation.GetDeferral();
            //TODO: Save application state and stop any background activity
            deferral.Complete();
        }
    }
}
```

Don't worry about the rest of this class for the moment. I'll return to it in Chapter 5 when I explain how to respond to the life cycle for Windows apps.

Writing the Code

The easiest way for me to explain how I have created the example app is to present the content in reverse order to the way you would usually create it in a project. To this end, I am going to start with the ListPage.xaml.cs code-behind file. You can see the contents of this file, with my additions to the Visual Studio default content, in Listing 2-4.

Listing 2-4. The ListPage.xaml.cs File

```
using GrocerApp.Data;
using Windows.UI.Xaml.Controls;
using Windows.UI.Xaml.Navigation;

namespace GrocerApp.Pages {

    public sealed partial class ListPage : Page {
        ViewModel viewModel;

        public ListPage() {

            viewModel = new ViewModel();

            viewModel.StoreList.Add("Whole Foods");
            viewModel.StoreList.Add("Kroger");
            viewModel.StoreList.Add("Costco");
            viewModel.StoreList.Add("Walmart");

            viewModel.GroceryList.Add(new GroceryItem {
                Name = "Apples",
                Quantity = 4, Store = "Whole Foods"
            });
            viewModel.GroceryList.Add(new GroceryItem {
                Name = "Hotdogs",
                Quantity = 12, Store = "Costco"
            });
            viewModel.GroceryList.Add(new GroceryItem {
                Name = "Soda",
                Quantity = 2, Store = "Costco"
            });
            viewModel.GroceryList.Add(new GroceryItem {
                Name = "Eggs",
                Quantity = 12, Store = "Kroger"
            });

            this.InitializeComponent();

            this.DataContext = viewModel;
        }

        protected override void OnNavigatedTo(NavigationEventArgs e) {
        }
```

```
        private void ListSelectionChanged(object sender,
            SelectionChangedEventArgs e) {
            viewModel.SelectedItemIndex = groceryList.SelectedIndex;
        }
    }
}
```

▓ **Caution**   You will get an error if you compile the app at this point because I refer to a
groceryList control that I have yet to add. You should wait until the "Running the App"
section; that's when everything will be in place.

The constructor for the ListPage class creates a new ViewModel object and populates
it with some sample data. The most interesting statement in this class is this:

this.DataContext = viewModel;

At the heart of the Windows app UI controls is support for *data binding* through
which I can display content from the view model in UI controls. To do this, I have
to specify the source of my data. The DataContext property specifies the source for
binding data for a UI control and all of its children. I can use the this keyword to set the
DataContext for the entire layout because the ListPage class consists of the contents of
the code-behind merged with the XAML content, meaning that this refers to the Page
object that contains all of the XAML-declared controls.

The final addition I made is to define a method that will handle the
SelectionChanged changed event from a ListView control. This is the kind of control
that I will used to display the items in the grocery list. When I define the XAML, I will
arrange things so that this method is invoked when the user selects one of those items.
This method sets the SelectedItemIndex property in the view model based on the
SelectedIndex property from the ListView control. Since the SelectedItemIndex
property is observable, other parts of my app can be notified when the user makes
a selection.

Adding a Resource Dictionary

In Chapter 1, I explained that the StandardStyles.xaml file created by Visual Studio
defines some XAML styles and templates that are used in Windows apps. Defining styles
like this is a good idea because it means you can apply changes in a single place, rather
than having to track down all of the places you applied a color or font setting directly to UI
controls. I need a few standard styles and templates for my example project. To this end, I
created a new folder called Resources and a new file called GrocerResourceDictionary.
xaml using the Resource Dictionary item template. You can see the contents of this file in
Listing 2-5.

■ **Tip**   As I explained in Chapter 1, Microsoft prohibits adding styles to `StandardStyles.xaml`. You must create your own resource dictionary if you want to create custom styles.

Listing 2-5. Defining a Resource Dictionary

```
<ResourceDictionary
    xmlns="http://schemas.microsoft.com/winfx/2006/xaml/presentation"
    xmlns:x="http://schemas.microsoft.com/winfx/2006/xaml"
    xmlns:local="using:GrocerApp.Resources">

    <ResourceDictionary.MergedDictionaries>
        <ResourceDictionary Source="/Common/StandardStyles.xaml" />
    </ResourceDictionary.MergedDictionaries>

    <SolidColorBrush x:Key="AppBackgroundColor" Color="#3E790A"/>

    <Style x:Key="GroceryListItem" TargetType="TextBlock"
            BasedOn="{StaticResource BasicTextStyle}" >
        <Setter Property="FontSize" Value="45"/>
        <Setter Property="FontWeight" Value="Light"/>
        <Setter Property="Margin" Value="10, 0"/>
        <Setter Property="VerticalAlignment" Value="Center"/>
    </Style>

    <DataTemplate x:Key="GroceryListItemTemplate">
        <StackPanel Orientation="Horizontal">
            <TextBlock Text="{Binding Quantity}"
                        Style="{StaticResource GroceryListItem}" Width="50"/>
            <TextBlock Text="{Binding Name}"
                        Style="{StaticResource GroceryListItem}"  Width="200"/>
            <TextBlock Text="{Binding Store}"
                        Style="{StaticResource GroceryListItem}"  Width="300"/>
        </StackPanel>
    </DataTemplate>

</ResourceDictionary>
```

I don't get into the detail of styles and templates in this book, but I will explain what I have done in this file since it will provide some context for later listings. The simplest declaration is this one:

```
...
<SolidColorBrush x:Key="AppBackgroundColor" Color="#3E790A"/>
...
```

The default color scheme for apps is white on black, which I want to change. The first step in changing this is to define a different color, which is what this element does, associating a shade of green with the key AppBackgroundColor. You will see me apply this color using its key when I create the XAML layout in a moment.

The next declaration is for a style, which consists of values for multiple properties:

```
...
<Style x:Key="GroceryListItem" TargetType="TextBlock"
    BasedOn="{StaticResource BasicTextStyle}" >
    <Setter Property="FontSize" Value="45"/>
    <Setter Property="FontWeight" Value="Light"/>
    <Setter Property="Margin" Value="10, 0"/>
    <Setter Property="VerticalAlignment" Value="Center"/>
</Style>
...
```

This style, which is called GroceryListItem, defines values for several properties: FontSize, FontWeight, and so on. But notice that I have used the BasedOn attribute when declaring the style. This allows me to inherit all of the values defined in another style. In this case, I inherit from the BasicTextStyle style that Microsoft defined in the StandardStyles.xaml file. I must bring other resource dictionary files into scope before I can derive new styles like this, which I do using this declaration:

```
<ResourceDictionary.MergedDictionaries>
    <ResourceDictionary Source="/Common/StandardStyles.xaml" />
</ResourceDictionary.MergedDictionaries>
```

You can import as many files as you like in this manner, but the import must happen before you derive styles from the files' content.

The final declaration is for a data template, with which I can define a hierarchy of elements that will be used to represent each item in a data source. As you might guess, my source of data will be the collection of grocery items in the view model. Each item in the collection will be represented by a StackPanel that contains three TextBlock controls. Notice the two attributes marked in bold:

```
...
<DataTemplate x:Key="GroceryListItemTemplate">
    <StackPanel Orientation="Horizontal">
        <TextBlock Text="{Binding Quantity}"
            Style="{StaticResource GroceryListItem}" Width="50"/>
        <TextBlock Text="{Binding Name}"
            Style="{StaticResource GroceryListItem}"  Width="200"/>
        <TextBlock Text="{Binding Store}"
            Style="{StaticResource GroceryListItem}"  Width="300"/>
    </StackPanel>
</DataTemplate>
...
```

The value of the Text attribute is important. The Binding keyword tells the runtime that I want the value of the Text attribute to be obtained from the DataContext for the control. In the previous section, I specified the view model as the source for this data, and specifying Quantity tells the runtime I want to use the Quantity property of the object that template is being used to display. By setting the DataContext property in the code-behind file, I specify the big picture ("use my view model of the source of binding data"), and the Binding keyword lets me specify the fine detail ("display the value of this particular property"). When I come to the main XAML file, I'll be able to connect the two so that the runtime knows which part of the view model should be used to get individual property values.

The other attribute I marked is less interesting but still useful. For the Style attribute, I have specified that I want a StaticResource called the GroceryList item. The StaticResource keyword tells the runtime that the resource I am looking for has already been defined. I have used the GroceryListItem style I specified a moment ago. The benefit here is that I can change the appearance of my three TextBlock controls in one place and that I can easily derive new styles for controls that I want to have a similar appearance. The last step is to add the custom resource dictionary to App.xaml so that it becomes available in the app, which I do in Listing 2-6.

Listing 2-6. Adding the Custom Resource Dictionary to the App.xaml File

```
<Application
    x:Class = "GrocerApp.App"
    xmlns = "http://schemas.microsoft.com/winfx/2006/xaml/presentation"
    xmlns:x = "http://schemas.microsoft.com/winfx/2006/xaml"
    xmlns:local = "using:GrocerApp">

    <Application.Resources>
        <ResourceDictionary>
            <ResourceDictionary.MergedDictionaries>

                <!--
                    Styles that define common aspects of the platform look and feel
                    Required by Visual Studio project and item templates
                -->
                <ResourceDictionary Source = "Common/StandardStyles.xaml"/>
                <ResourceDictionary Source = "Resources/
                                            GrocerResourceDictionary.xaml"/>
            </ResourceDictionary.MergedDictionaries>

        </ResourceDictionary>
    </Application.Resources>
</Application>
```

Writing the XAML

Now that I have the code-behind file and the resource dictionary in place, I can turn to the XAML to declare the controls that will form the app layout. Listing 2-7 shows the content of the ListPage.xaml file.

Listing 2-7. The ListPage.xaml File

```xml
<Page
    x:Class = "GrocerApp.Pages.ListPage"
    xmlns = "http://schemas.microsoft.com/winfx/2006/xaml/presentation"
    xmlns:x = "http://schemas.microsoft.com/winfx/2006/xaml"
    xmlns:local = "using:GrocerApp.Pages"
    xmlns:d = "http://schemas.microsoft.com/expression/blend/2008"
    xmlns:mc = "http://schemas.openxmlformats.org/markup-compatibility/2006"
    mc:Ignorable = "d">

    <Grid Background = "{StaticResource AppBackgroundColor}">

        <Grid.RowDefinitions>
            <RowDefinition/>
            <RowDefinition/>
        </Grid.RowDefinitions>
        <Grid.ColumnDefinitions>
            <ColumnDefinition/>
            <ColumnDefinition/>
        </Grid.ColumnDefinitions>

        <StackPanel Grid.RowSpan="2">

            <TextBlock Style="{StaticResource HeaderTextStyle}" Margin="10"
                    Text="Grocery List"/>
            <ListView x:Name="groceryList" Grid.RowSpan="2"
                ItemsSource="{Binding GroceryList}"
                ItemTemplate="{StaticResource GroceryListItemTemplate}"
                SelectionChanged="ListSelectionChanged" />
        </StackPanel>

        <StackPanel Orientation="Vertical" Grid.Column="1">
            <TextBlock Style="{StaticResource HeaderTextStyle}" Margin="10"
                    Text="Item Detail"/>
        </StackPanel>

        <StackPanel Orientation="Vertical" Grid.Column="1" Grid.Row="1">
            <TextBlock Style="{StaticResource HeaderTextStyle}" Margin="10"
                    Text="Store Detail"/>
        </StackPanel>

    </Grid>
</Page>
```

You can see that I have set the Background attribute for the Grid control to the color
I specified in the resource dictionary. In addition, I configured the Grid control that was

defined by Visual Studio and divided it into two equal-sized columns, each of which has two equal-sized rows using the `Grid.RowDefinitions` and `Grid.ColumnDefinitions` elements.

For the left side of the layout, I have added a `StackPanel` that I have configured so that it spans two rows and fills the left half of the layout:

```
...
<StackPanel Grid.RowSpan="2">
...
```

This `StackPanel` contains a `TextBlock`, which I use to display a header, and a `ListView`, which I'll come back to shortly. For the right side of the screen, I have added a pair of `StackPanels`, one in each row. I have specified which row and column each belongs in using the `Grid.Row` and `Grid.Column` attributes. These attributes use a zero-based index, and controls that don't have these attributes are put in the first row and column. You can see how the layout appears on the Visual Studio design surface in Figure 2-1.

Figure 2-1. *The static parts of the XAML layout displayed on the Visual Studio design surface*

The design surface isn't able to display content that is generated dynamically, which is why you can't see the view model data in the figure. The dynamic content will be displayed in a `ListView` control. As its name suggests, `ListView` displays a set of items in a list. There are three XAML attributes that set out how this will be done:

```
...
<ListView x:Name="groceryList" Grid.RowSpan="2"
    ItemsSource="{Binding GroceryList}"
```

```
ItemTemplate = "{StaticResource GroceryListItemTemplate}"
SelectionChanged = "ListSelectionChanged" />
...
```

I use these properties to close the gap between the macro-level DataContext property and the micro-level properties in the template. The ItemSource attribute tells the ListView control where it should get the set of items it must display. The Binding keyword with a value of GroceryList tells the ListView that it should display the contents of the GroceryList property of the DataContext object I set in the code-behind file.

The ItemTemplate attribute tells the ListView how each item from the ItemSource should be displayed. The StaticResource keyword and the GroceryListItemTemplate value mean that the data template I specified in the resource dictionary will be used, meaning that a new StackPanel containing three TextBlock elements will be generated for each item in the ViewModel.GroceryList collection.

The final attribute is associated with the event handler method I defined in the code-behind file with the SelectionChanged event emitted by the ListView control.

■ **Tip**   You can get a list of the events that the controls define using the Visual Studio Properties window or by consulting the Microsoft API documentation. The easiest way to create handler methods with the right arguments is to let the XAML editor create them for you as part of the autocomplete process.

Running the App

The Visual Studio design surface can display only the parts of the layout that are static. The only way to see the dynamic content is to run the app. So, to see the way that the XAML and the C# come together, select Start Debugging from the Visual Studio Debug menu. Visual Studio will build the project and push the app to the simulator. You can see the result in Figure 2-2.

Figure 2-2. *Running the example app in the simulator*

You can see how the data binding adds items from the view model to the `ListView` control and how the template I defined in the resource dictionary has been used to format them.

There is a lot of built-in behavior with the Windows app UI controls. For example, items are shown in a lighter shade when the mouse moves over them (which you can see in Figure 2-2) and in a different shade when the user clicks to select an item. All of the styles used by a control can be changed, but I am going to stick with the default settings for simplicity.

Inserting Other Pages into the Layout

You don't have to put all of your controls and code in a single XAML file and its code-behind file. To make a project easier to manage, you can create multiple pages and bring them together in your app. As a simple demonstration, I have created a new `Blank Page` called `NoItemSelected.xaml` in my `Pages` project folder. Listing 2-8 shows the content of this file with my additions to the default content shown in bold.

■ **Tip** You will have to stop the debugger before Visual Studio will let you add new items to the project.

35

Listing 2-8. The NoItemSelected.xaml File

```
<Page
    x:Class="GrocerApp.Pages.NoItemSelected"
    xmlns="http://schemas.microsoft.com/winfx/2006/xaml/presentation"
    xmlns:x="http://schemas.microsoft.com/winfx/2006/xaml"
    xmlns:local="using:GrocerApp.Pages"
    xmlns:d="http://schemas.microsoft.com/expression/blend/2008"
    xmlns:mc="http://schemas.openxmlformats.org/markup-compatibility/2006"
    mc:Ignorable="d">

    <Grid Background="{StaticResource AppBackgroundColor}">
        <TextBlock Style="{StaticResource HeaderTextStyle}"
                   FontSize="30" Text="No Item Selected"/>
    </Grid>
</Page>
```

This is a very simple page—so simple that you wouldn't usually need to create a page like this because it just displays some static text. But it is helpful to demonstrate an important app feature, allowing me to break up my app into manageable pieces. The key to adding pages to my main app layout is the Frame control, which I have added to the ListPage.xaml layout, as shown in Listing 2-9.

Listing 2-9. Adding a Frame Control to the App Layout

```
<Page
    x:Class="GrocerApp.Pages.ListPage"
    xmlns="http://schemas.microsoft.com/winfx/2006/xaml/presentation"
    xmlns:x="http://schemas.microsoft.com/winfx/2006/xaml"
    xmlns:local="using:GrocerApp.Pages"
    xmlns:d="http://schemas.microsoft.com/expression/blend/2008"
    xmlns:mc="http://schemas.openxmlformats.org/markup-compatibility/2006"
    mc:Ignorable="d">

    <Grid Background="{StaticResource AppBackgroundColor}">

        <Grid.RowDefinitions>
            <RowDefinition/>
            <RowDefinition/>
        </Grid.RowDefinitions>
        <Grid.ColumnDefinitions>
            <ColumnDefinition/>
            <ColumnDefinition/>
        </Grid.ColumnDefinitions>

        <StackPanel Grid.RowSpan="2">

            <TextBlock Style="{StaticResource HeaderTextStyle}" Margin="10"
                       Text="Grocery List"/>
```

```xml
            <ListView x:Name="groceryList" Grid.RowSpan="2"
                ItemsSource="{Binding GroceryList}"
                ItemTemplate="{StaticResource GroceryListItemTemplate}"
                SelectionChanged="ListSelectionChanged" />
        </StackPanel>

        <StackPanel Orientation="Vertical" Grid.Column="1">
            <TextBlock Style="{StaticResource HeaderTextStyle}" Margin="10"
                    Text="Item Detail"/>
            <Frame x:Name="ItemDetailFrame"/>
        </StackPanel>

        <StackPanel Orientation="Vertical" Grid.Column="1" Grid.Row="1">
            <TextBlock Style="{StaticResource HeaderTextStyle}" Margin="10"
                    Text="Store Detail"/>
        </StackPanel>
    </Grid>
</Page>
```

A Frame is a placeholder for a Page, and I use the Navigate method in my ListPage.xaml.cs code-behind file to tell the Frame which page I want it to display, as Listing 2-10 shows.

Listing 2-10. Specifying the Page Shown by a Frame in the ListPage.xaml.cs File

```csharp
using GrocerApp.Data;
using Windows.UI.Xaml.Controls;
using Windows.UI.Xaml.Navigation;

namespace GrocerApp.Pages {

    public sealed partial class ListPage : Page {
        ViewModel viewModel;

        public ListPage() {

            viewModel = new ViewModel();

            // ... test data removed for brevity

            this.InitializeComponent();

            this.DataContext = viewModel;

            ItemDetailFrame.Navigate(typeof(NoItemSelected));
        }
```

```
        protected override void OnNavigatedTo(NavigationEventArgs e) {
        }

        private void ListSelectionChanged(object sender,
            SelectionChangedEventArgs e) {
            viewModel.SelectedItemIndex = groceryList.SelectedIndex;
        }
    }
}
```

The argument to the Navigate method is a System.Type representing the Page class
you want to load, and the easiest way to get a System.Type is with the typeof keyword.
The Navigate method instantiates the Page object (remember that XAML and the
code-behind file are combined to create a single subclass of Page), and the result is
inserted into the layout, as shown in Figure 2-3.

Figure 2-3. *Inserting another page into the layout*

Dynamically Inserting Pages into the Layout

You can also use a Frame to dynamically insert different pages into your layout based on
the state of your app. To demonstrate this, I have created a new Blank Page in the Pages
folder called ItemDetail.xaml, the contents of which are shown in Listing 2-11. (This file
relies on styles from my custom dictionary; you can see how I defined them in the source
code download for this chapter.)

Listing 2-11. The ItemDetail.xaml Page

```
<Page
    x:Class = "GrocerApp.Pages.ItemDetail"
    xmlns = "http://schemas.microsoft.com/winfx/2006/xaml/presentation"
    xmlns:x = "http://schemas.microsoft.com/winfx/2006/xaml"
    xmlns:local = "using:GrocerApp.Pages"
    xmlns:d = "http://schemas.microsoft.com/expression/blend/2008"
    xmlns:mc = "http://schemas.openxmlformats.org/markup-compatibility/2006"
    mc:Ignorable = "d">

    <Grid Background = "{StaticResource AppBackgroundColor}">
```

```
    <Grid.RowDefinitions>
        <RowDefinition Height="Auto" />
        <RowDefinition Height="Auto"/>
        <RowDefinition Height="Auto"/>
    </Grid.RowDefinitions>
    <Grid.ColumnDefinitions>
        <ColumnDefinition Width="Auto"/>
        <ColumnDefinition Width="*"/>
    </Grid.ColumnDefinitions>

    <TextBlock Text="Name:" Style="{StaticResource ItemDetailText}" />
    <TextBlock Text="Quantity:" Style="{StaticResource ItemDetailText}"
            Grid.Row="1"/>
    <TextBlock Text="Store:" Style="{StaticResource ItemDetailText}"
            Grid.Row="2"/>

    <TextBox x:Name="ItemDetailName"
            Style="{StaticResource ItemDetailTextBox}"
            TextChanged="HandleItemChange"
            Grid.Column="1"/>

    <TextBox x:Name="ItemDetailQuantity"
            Style="{StaticResource ItemDetailTextBox}"
            TextChanged="HandleItemChange"
            Grid.Row="1" Grid.Column="1"/>

    <ComboBox x:Name="ItemDetailStore"
            Style="{StaticResource ItemDetailStore}"
            Grid.Column="1" Grid.Row="2"
            ItemsSource="{Binding StoreList}"
            SelectionChanged="HandleItemChange"
            DisplayMemberPath="" />
    </Grid>
</Page>
```

The layout for this Page is based around a grid, with text labels and input controls to allow the user to edit the details of an item on the grocery list, the details of which I'll set in the code-behind file shortly.

■ **Tip**　I use a ComboBox control to present the list of stores to the user, which I populate directly from the view model. I have set the ItemSource attribute so that the control binds to the StoreList property in the view model, but the ComboBox control expects to be told which property should be displayed from the collection of objects it is working with. Since my list of stores is just an array of strings, I have to work around this by setting the DisplayMemberPath attribute to the empty string.

I need to define some new styles in my Resources/GrocerResourceDictionary.xaml file, which you can see in Listing 2-12.

Listing 2-12. Adding Styles to the Resource Dictionary

```
<ResourceDictionary
    xmlns="http://schemas.microsoft.com/winfx/2006/xaml/presentation"
    xmlns:x="http://schemas.microsoft.com/winfx/2006/xaml"
    xmlns:local="using:GrocerApp.Resources">

    <ResourceDictionary.MergedDictionaries>
        <ResourceDictionary Source="/Common/StandardStyles.xaml" />
    </ResourceDictionary.MergedDictionaries>

    <!-- ...previous styles ommitted for brevity... -->

    <Style x:Key="ItemDetailText" TargetType="TextBlock"
            BasedOn="{StaticResource GroceryListItem}" >
        <Setter Property="FontSize" Value="35"/>
        <Setter Property="HorizontalAlignment" Value="Right"/>
    </Style>

    <Style x:Key="ItemDetailTextBox" TargetType="TextBox" >
        <Setter Property="FontSize" Value="30"/>
        <Setter Property="Margin" Value="10"/>
    </Style>

    <Style x:Key="ItemDetailStore" TargetType="ComboBox">
        <Setter Property="Foreground" Value="Black"/>
        <Setter Property="Height" Value="55"/>
        <Setter Property="FontSize" Value="30"/>
        <Setter Property="VerticalAlignment" Value="Top"/>
        <Setter Property="Margin" Value="10"/>
    </Style>

</ResourceDictionary>
```

Switching Between Pages

Now that I have two pages, I can switch between them as the state of my app changes. I am going to display the NoItemSelected page when the user hasn't selected an item from the ListView and the ItemDetail page when the user has made a selection. Listing 2-13 shows the additions to the ListPage.xaml.cs file that make this happen.

Listing 2-13. Showing Pages Based on App State

```
...
public ListPage() {

    viewModel = new ViewModel();

    // ...test data removed for brevity

    this.InitializeComponent();

    this.DataContext = viewModel;

    ItemDetailFrame.Navigate(typeof(NoItemSelected));

    viewModel.PropertyChanged += (sender, args) => {
        if (args.PropertyName == "SelectedItemIndex") {
            if (viewModel.SelectedItemIndex == -1) {
                ItemDetailFrame.Navigate(typeof(NoItemSelected));
            } else {
                ItemDetailFrame.Navigate(typeof(ItemDetail), viewModel);
            }
        }
    };
}
...
```

I still display the NoItemSelected page by default, because that reflects the initial state of my app. The user won't have made a selection when the app first starts.

The additional code adds a handler for the PropertyChanged event defined by the view model. This is the same event that is used by the XAML controls data binding feature, and by registering a handler directly, I am able to respond to property changes in the view model in my code-behind file. The event arguments I receive when I handle this event tell me which property has changed through the PropertyName property. If the SelectedItemIndex property has changed, then I use the Frame.Navigate method to show either the NoItemSelected or ItemDetail page.

Notice that I pass the view model object as an argument to the Navigate method when I display the ItemDetail page:

```
ItemDetailFrame.Navigate(typeof(ItemDetail), viewModel);
```

This argument is the means by which you can pass context to the page that is being displayed. I'll show you how to use this object in the next section.

Implementing the Embedded Page

Of course, it isn't enough just to define the XAML for my `ItemDetail` page. I also have to write the code that will display the details of the selected item and allow the user to make changes. Listing 2-14 shows the `ItemDetail.xaml.cs` code-behind file, which does just this.

Listing 2-14. The ItemDetail.xaml.cs Code-Behind File

```
using GrocerApp.Data;
using System;
using Windows.UI.Xaml;
using Windows.UI.Xaml.Controls;
using Windows.UI.Xaml.Navigation;

namespace GrocerApp.Pages {

    public sealed partial class ItemDetail : Page {
        private ViewModel viewModel;

        public ItemDetail() {
            this.InitializeComponent();
        }

        protected override void OnNavigatedTo(NavigationEventArgs e) {

            viewModel = e.Parameter as ViewModel;
            this.DataContext = viewModel;

            viewModel.PropertyChanged += (sender, eventArgs) => {
                if (eventArgs.PropertyName == "SelectedItemIndex") {
                    if (viewModel.SelectedItemIndex == -1) {
                        SetItemDetail(null);
                    } else {
                        SetItemDetail(viewModel.GroceryList
                            [viewModel.SelectedItemIndex]);
                    }
                }
            };
            SetItemDetail(viewModel.GroceryList[viewModel.SelectedItemIndex]);
        }

        private void SetItemDetail(GroceryItem item) {
            ItemDetailName.Text = (item == null) ? "" : item.Name;
            ItemDetailQuantity.Text = (item == null) ? ""
                : item.Quantity.ToString();
```

```
            if (item != null) {
                ItemDetailStore.SelectedItem = item.Store;
            } else {
                ItemDetailStore.SelectedIndex = -1;
            }
        }

        private void HandleItemChange(object sender, RoutedEventArgs e) {
            if (viewModel.SelectedItemIndex > -1) {

                GroceryItem selectedItem = viewModel.GroceryList
                    [viewModel.SelectedItemIndex];

                if (sender == ItemDetailName) {
                    selectedItem.Name = ItemDetailName.Text;

                } else if (sender == ItemDetailQuantity) {
                    int intVal;
                    bool parsed = Int32.TryParse(ItemDetailQuantity.Text,
                        out intVal);
                    if (parsed) {
                        selectedItem.Quantity = intVal;
                    }
                } else if (sender == ItemDetailStore) {
                    string store = (String)((ComboBox)sender).SelectedItem;

                    if (store != null) {
                        viewModel.GroceryList
                            [viewModel.SelectedItemIndex].Store = store;
                    }
                }
            }
        }
    }
}
```

The SetItemDetail method sets the content of the UI controls to display the details of the selected grocery list item, and the HandleItemChange method updates that item when the user changes the contents of one of the controls.

The interesting part of this listing is the OnNavigatedTo method, which I have marked in bold in the listing. This method is called when the ItemDetail page is displayed, and the object that I passed to the Frame.Navigate model is available through the Parameter property of the event arguments. You can see the ItemDetail page in the layout in Figure 2-4.

Figure 2-4. *Displaying the ItemDetail page*

By passing the view model object around in this way, I am able to ensure that all of my pages are working with the same data, while being able to break down the app into manageable portions.

Summary

In this chapter, I showed you how to create a view model in a Windows app and make it observable so that you can use data binding to keep the layout of your app synchronized with the view model data. This is an essential technique for creating robust and easily maintained apps. I also showed you how you can break down your app into manageable chunks by creating pages and how you can use a Frame to display those pages as part of your main layout. In the next chapter, I'll show you how to create some of the most important controls for a Windows app: the AppBar, the NavBar, and flyouts.

CHAPTER 3

■ ■ ■

AppBars, Flyouts, and Navigation

In this chapter, I show you how to create and use some of the user interactions that are essential parts of the Windows app user experience. The Application Bar (AppBar) and Navigation Bar (NavBar) provide the means by which the user can interact with your content and features and navigate within your app. I also show you how to create flyouts, which are pop-ups used to capture information from the user, usually in response to an interaction with the AppBar. Table 3-1 provides the summary for this chapter.

Table 3-1. *Chapter Summary*

Problem	Solution	Listing
Add an AppBar.	Declare an AppBar control within the XAML Page.BottomAppBar property.	1
Add buttons to an AppBar.	Use Button controls, formatted either with predefined or with custom styles.	2–5
Add a flyout.	Declare a Popup control with the IsLightDismissEnabled property set to True.	6, 8
Display a flyout.	Position the Popup relative to the AppBar Button that caused it to be displayed.	9–11
Easily obtain access to the view model for a flyout.	Use the DataContext property.	12–15
Add a NavBar.	Create a wrapper Page that declares an AppBar element within the XAML Page.TopAppBar property.	16, 18
Navigate within an App.	Add a Frame control to the wrapper Page and use the Navigate method to show other Page controls when the NavBar buttons are clicked.	19

Adding an AppBar

The *AppBar* appears at the bottom of the screen when the user makes an upward-swiping gesture or right-clicks with the mouse. The emphasis in the Windows 8 app UI is to have few extraneous controls in the main layout and to rely on the AppBar as the mechanism for any interaction that is not about the immediately available functionality but that *does* pertain to the currently displayed layout. In this section, I'll show you how to define and populate an AppBar.

▦ **Tip** There is a similar control at the top of the screen, called the Navigation Bar (NavBar), which is used to navigate between different parts of an app. I show you how to create and use the NavBar later in this chapter.

Declaring the AppBar

The simplest way to create an AppBar is to declare it in your XAML file. Listing 3-1 shows the additions to the ListPage.xaml file from the example project.

Listing 3-1. Defining an AppBar

```
<Page
    x:Class="GrocerApp.Pages.ListPage"
    xmlns="http://schemas.microsoft.com/winfx/2006/xaml/presentation"
    xmlns:x="http://schemas.microsoft.com/winfx/2006/xaml"
    xmlns:local="using:GrocerApp.Pages"
    xmlns:d="http://schemas.microsoft.com/expression/blend/2008"
    xmlns:mc="http://schemas.openxmlformats.org/markup-compatibility/2006"
    mc:Ignorable="d">

    <Grid Background="{StaticResource AppBackgroundColor}">

        <Grid.RowDefinitions>
            <RowDefinition/>
            <RowDefinition/>
        </Grid.RowDefinitions>
        <Grid.ColumnDefinitions>
            <ColumnDefinition/>
            <ColumnDefinition/>
        </Grid.ColumnDefinitions>

        <StackPanel Grid.RowSpan="2">

            <TextBlock Style="{StaticResource HeaderTextStyle}" Margin="10"
                    Text="Grocery List"/>
            <ListView x:Name="groceryList" Grid.RowSpan="2"
                ItemsSource="{Binding GroceryList}"
```

```
          ItemTemplate="{StaticResource GroceryListItemTemplate}"
          SelectionChanged="ListSelectionChanged" />
    </StackPanel>

    <StackPanel Orientation="Vertical" Grid.Column="1">
        <TextBlock Style="{StaticResource HeaderTextStyle}" Margin="10"
                Text="Item Detail"/>
        <Frame x:Name="ItemDetailFrame"/>
    </StackPanel>

    <StackPanel Orientation="Vertical" Grid.Column="1" Grid.Row="1">
        <TextBlock Style="{StaticResource HeaderTextStyle}" Margin="10"
                Text="Store Detail"/>
    </StackPanel>
</Grid>

<Page.BottomAppBar>
    <AppBar>
        <Grid>
            <Grid.ColumnDefinitions>
                <ColumnDefinition />
                <ColumnDefinition />
            </Grid.ColumnDefinitions>

            <StackPanel Orientation="Horizontal" Grid.Column="0"
                    HorizontalAlignment="Left">
                <Button x:Name="AppBarDoneButton"
                        Style="{StaticResource DoneAppBarButtonStyle}"
                        IsEnabled="false"
                        Click="AppBarButtonClick"/>
            </StackPanel>

            <StackPanel Orientation="Horizontal" Grid.Column="1"
                    HorizontalAlignment="Right">

                <Button x:Name="AppBarAddButton"
                        Style="{StaticResource AddAppBarButtonStyle}"
                        AutomationProperties.Name="New Item"
                        Click="AppBarButtonClick"/>

                <Button x:Name="AppBarStoresButton"
                        Style="{StaticResource StoresAppBarButton}"
                        Click="AppBarButtonClick"/>

                <Button x:Name="AppBarZipButton"
                        Style="{StaticResource HomeAppBarButtonStyle}"
                        AutomationProperties.Name="Zip Code"
                        Click="AppBarButtonClick"/>
```

```
            </StackPanel>
        </Grid>
    </AppBar>
  </Page.BottomAppBar>
</Page>
```

To create the AppBar, I have to declare an AppBar control within the Page.BottomAppBar property, as shown in the listing. This has the effect of creating the AppBar and its contents and assigning them to the BottomAppBar property of the containing page.

■ **Tip**   You can create the NavBar by declaring an AppBar control within the Page.TopAppBar property.

AppBars contain buttons, and the convention is to have buttons that are specified to the currently selected item shown on the left side of the AppBar and app-wide buttons shown on the right. To follow this convention, I have added a Grid to my AppBar control. The Grid has one row and two columns, and each column contains a StackPanel.

There are two ways to add buttons to an AppBar: you can select and adapt ones that are already defined in StandardStyles.xaml, or you can create your own. The listing uses both approaches, which I explain in the following sections.

Adapting Predefined AppBar Buttons

Most of the /Common/StandardStyles.xaml file, which is added to Visual Studio projects automatically when they are created, contains styles for Button controls that are part of an AppBar, like the one shown in Listing 3-2.

■ **Note**   There are a lot of these button styles in the StandardStyles.xaml file, and, by default, they are commented out. This means you have to uncomment the ones you want to use. For this chapter, you will need to search for HomeAppBarButtonStyle and AddAppBarButtonStyle and uncomment them; otherwise, they won't be available for use in the example app.

Listing 3-2. The Style for the Add AppBar Button

```
...
<Style x:Key="AddAppBarButtonStyle" TargetType="ButtonBase"
        BasedOn="{StaticResource AppBarButtonStyle}">
    <Setter Property="AutomationProperties.AutomationId"
Value="AddAppBarButton"/>
```

```
    <Setter Property="AutomationProperties.Name" Value="Add"/>
    <Setter Property="Content" Value="&#xE109;"/>
</Style>
...
```

All of the predefined Button styles are derived from the AppBarButtonStyle, which defines the basic characteristics of an AppBar button. I'll use this style when I create my own button in the next section.

The two properties that differentiate individual buttons are AutomationProperties. Name and Content. The AutomationProperties.Name property specifies the text shown under the button, and the Context property specifies the icon that will be used. The value for this property is a character code from the Segoe UI Symbol font. You can see the icons defined by this font using the Character Map tool that is included in Windows 8; the value E109 corresponds to a plus sign.

The style shown in the listing doesn't quite meet my needs. I like the icon, but I want to change the text. To adapt the button to my needs in the ListPage.xaml file, I simply use the predefined style and override the parts I want to change, as shown in Listing 3-3.

Listing 3-3. Adapting a Predefined AppBar Button in the LisPage.xaml File

```
...
<Button x:Name="AppBarAddButton"
    Style="{StaticResource AddAppBarButtonStyle}"
    AutomationProperties.Name="New Item"
    Click="AppBarButtonClick"/>
...
```

Creating Custom AppBar Button Styles

An alternative approach is to define your own styles for your AppBar buttons. Listing 3-4 shows a style I added to my resource /Resources/GrocerResourceDictionary.xaml file for this purpose.

Listing 3-4. Defining a Custom AppBar Button Styles

```
...
<Style x:Key="StoresAppBarButton" TargetType="Button"
        BasedOn="{StaticResource AppBarButtonStyle}">
    <Setter Property="AutomationProperties.Name" Value="Stores"/>
    <Setter Property="Content" Value="&#xE14D;"/>
</Style>

<Style x:Key="DoneAppBarButtonStyle" TargetType="Button"
        BasedOn="{StaticResource AppBarButtonStyle}">
    <Setter Property="AutomationProperties.Name" Value="Done"/>
    <Setter Property="Content" Value="&#xE10B;"/>
</Style>
...
```

I have based these styles on `AppBarButtonStyle`, so I get the basic look and feel for an AppBar button, and I have set values for the `AutomationProperties.Name` and `Content` properties. You can go further and redefine some of the core characteristics of the underlying style, but you run the risk of departing from the standard Windows 8 app appearance and experience that your users will expect.

Implementing AppBar Button Actions

The `Button` controls on the AppBar don't do anything at the moment. To address this, I am going to implement the Done button, just so you can see how it is done.

I will activate this `Button` when the user makes a selection from the grocery item list. When the user clicks the button, I will remove the currently selected item from the list, allowing the user to indicate when they have purchased an item. Listing 3-5 shows the changes to the `ListPage.xaml.cs` code-behind file.

Listing 3-5. Implementing the Done AppBar Button

```
using GrocerApp.Data;
using Windows.UI.Xaml;
using Windows.UI.Xaml.Controls;
using Windows.UI.Xaml.Navigation;

namespace GrocerApp.Pages {

    public sealed partial class ListPage : Page {
        ViewModel viewModel;

        public ListPage() {

            viewModel = new ViewModel();

            // ...test data removed for brevity

            this.InitializeComponent();

            this.DataContext = viewModel;

            ItemDetailFrame.Navigate(typeof(NoItemSelected));

            viewModel.PropertyChanged += (sender, args) => {
                if (args.PropertyName == "SelectedItemIndex") {
                    if (viewModel.SelectedItemIndex == -1) {
                        ItemDetailFrame.Navigate(typeof(NoItemSelected));
                        AppBarDoneButton.IsEnabled = false;
                    } else {
                        ItemDetailFrame.Navigate(typeof(ItemDetail), viewModel);
                        AppBarDoneButton.IsEnabled = true;
                    }
```

```
                }
            };
    }

    protected override void OnNavigatedTo(NavigationEventArgs e) {
    }

    private void ListSelectionChanged(object sender,
        SelectionChangedEventArgs e) {
        viewModel.SelectedItemIndex = groceryList.SelectedIndex;
    }

    private void AppBarButtonClick(object sender, RoutedEventArgs e) {
        if (e.OriginalSource == AppBarDoneButton
                && viewModel.SelectedItemIndex > -1) {

            viewModel.GroceryList.RemoveAt(viewModel.SelectedItemIndex);
            viewModel.SelectedItemIndex = -1;
        }
    }
  }
}
```

There are two points to note in this listing. The first is that for simple tasks, implementing the action for a Button on the AppBar is just a matter of responding to the Click event.

The second point is that you can start to see the benefit of the view model appearing in the code. My code in the AppBarButtonClick method doesn't need to switch the contents of the Frame to the NoItemSelected page or that the Done button should be disabled when an item is completed. I just update the view model, and the rest of the app adapts to those changes to present the user with the right layout and overall experience.

You can see the result of adding the AppBar and its Button controls in Figure 3-1. If you want to see the AppBar firsthand, then start the example app and swipe from the top or bottom of the screen or right-click with the mouse. The figure shows both states of the Done button, which you can re=create by selecting an item from the list.

Figure 3-1. *Adding an AppBar to the example app*

Creating Flyouts

The Done AppBar button has a simple action associated with it, which can be performed directly in the event handler code associated with the Click event. Most AppBar buttons, however, require some kind of additional user interaction, and this is performed using a *flyout*.

A flyout is a pop-up window that is displayed near the AppBar button that has been clicked and that is dismissed automatically when the user clicks or touches elsewhere on the screen. There is a Flyout control for JavaScript Windows 8 apps, but getting the same effect with XAML and C# requires the use of a Popup and some careful positioning code.

Creating the User Control

XAML files can quickly become long and difficult to manage. I like to define my flyouts as *user controls*, which are like snippets of XAML elements and a code-behind file. (I am skipping some XAML details here, but you'll see what I mean as you read this section of the chapter.) I have created a folder in my example project called Flyouts and used the UserControl template to create a new item called HomeZipCodeFlyout.xaml, the contents of which you can see in Listing 3-6.

Listing 3-6. The HomeZipCodeFlyout.xaml File

```
<UserControl
    x:Class="GrocerApp.Flyouts.HomeZipCodeFlyout"
    xmlns="http://schemas.microsoft.com/winfx/2006/xaml/presentation"
    xmlns:x="http://schemas.microsoft.com/winfx/2006/xaml"
    xmlns:local="using:GrocerApp.Flyouts"
```

```
    xmlns:d="http://schemas.microsoft.com/expression/blend/2008"
    xmlns:mc="http://schemas.openxmlformats.org/markup-compatibility/2006"
    mc:Ignorable="d"
    d:DesignHeight="300"
    d:DesignWidth="400">

    <Popup x:Name="HomeZipCodePopup"
            IsLightDismissEnabled="True" Width="350" Height="130" >
        <StackPanel Background="Black">
            <Border Background="#85C54C" BorderThickness="4">
                <StackPanel>
                    <StackPanel Orientation="Horizontal" Margin="10">
                        <TextBlock Style="{StaticResource PopupTextStyle}"
                            Text="Home Zip Code:"
                                VerticalAlignment="Center"
                            Margin="0,0,10,0" />
                        <TextBox Height="40" Width="150" FontSize="20"
                                Text="{Binding Path=HomeZipCode,
                                    Mode=TwoWay}" />
                    </StackPanel>
                    <Button Click="OKButtonClick"
                        HorizontalAlignment="Center"
                            Margin="10">OK</Button>
                </StackPanel>
            </Border>
        </StackPanel>
    </Popup>
</UserControl>
```

As the file name suggests, this flyout will allow the user to change the value of the
HomeZipCode property in the view model. This property doesn't do anything in the
example, other than provide an opportunity for some useful examples.

User controls work like templates. Within the UserControl element, you define the
XAML elements that represent the controls you want to create. You must use a Popup
control when creating flyouts, but the content that you put inside the Popup is up to you.
My layout in the listing consists of a TextBox to collect the new value from the user, a
Button so that the user can indicate when they have entered the new value, and some
surrounding elements to provide context and structure.

There are three important attributes that you must set for your Popup element, each
of which I have marked in bold in the listing. The IsLightDismissEnabled attribute
specifies whether the pop-up will be dismissed if the user clicks or touches anywhere
outside of the Popup; this must be set to True when you are using Popups for flyouts
because it is an essential part of the flyout user experience.

The Width and Height attributes must be set so that the Popup is just large enough to
contain its contents. I need explicit values for these attributes when I position the Popup,
which I'll demonstrate shortly.

■ **Caution**   If you use my positioning code (which I describe shortly) to manage your flyouts, then you *must* provide explicit and accurate `Width` and `Height` values. The flyout won't be positioned correctly if you omit the values or provide inaccurate dimensions.

You will see that I reference the PopupTextStyle style in the listing. I defined this style, and some others that I need in this chapter, in my /Resources/ GrocerResourceDictionary file, as shown in Listing 3-7.

Listing 3-7. Defining a Custom Style for the Flyouts

```xml
<ResourceDictionary
    xmlns="http://schemas.microsoft.com/winfx/2006/xaml/presentation"
    xmlns:x="http://schemas.microsoft.com/winfx/2006/xaml"
    xmlns:local="using:GrocerApp.Resources">

    <ResourceDictionary.MergedDictionaries>
        <ResourceDictionary Source="/Common/StandardStyles.xaml" />
    </ResourceDictionary.MergedDictionaries>

    <!-- ...other styles omitted for brevity... -->

    <Style x:Key="PopupTextStyle" TargetType="TextBlock"
            BasedOn="{StaticResource BasicTextStyle}">
        <Setter Property="FontSize" Value="22" />
    </Style>

    <Style x:Key="AddItemText" TargetType="TextBlock"
            BasedOn="{StaticResource GroceryListItem}" >
        <Setter Property="FontSize" Value="22"/>
        <Setter Property="HorizontalAlignment" Value="Right"/>
        <Setter Property="VerticalAlignment" Value="Center"/>
    </Style>

    <Style x:Key="AddItemTextBox" TargetType="TextBox"
            BasedOn="{StaticResource ItemDetailTextBox}">
        <Setter Property="FontSize" Value="22"/>
    </Style>

    <Style x:Key="AddItemStore" TargetType="ComboBox"
            BasedOn="{StaticResource ItemDetailStore}">
        <Setter Property="FontSize" Value="22"/>
    </Style>

</ResourceDictionary>
```

Writing the User Control Code

User controls still have code-behind files, even though they present fragments of XAML. Listing 3-8 shows the contents of the HomeZipCodeFlyout.xaml.cs file.

Listing 3-8. The HomeZipCodeFlyout.xaml.cs File

```
using Windows.UI.Xaml;
using Windows.UI.Xaml.Controls;

namespace GrocerApp.Flyouts {
    public sealed partial class HomeZipCodeFlyout : UserControl {

        public HomeZipCodeFlyout() {
            this.InitializeComponent();
        }

        public void Show(Page page, AppBar appbar, Button button) {
            HomeZipCodePopup.IsOpen = true;
            FlyoutHelper.ShowRelativeToAppBar(HomeZipCodePopup, page,
            appbar, button);
        }

        private void OKButtonClick(object sender, RoutedEventArgs e) {
            HomeZipCodePopup.IsOpen = false;
        }
    }
}
```

The main problem I have to solve for my flyout is positioning the Popup. The convention for flyouts that appear in response to an AppBar button is to show the Popup just above the clicked Button element.

Positioning the Popup Control

The Windows app controls don't provide a simple way of working out the relative position of elements in the layout, so some indirect techniques are required. Listing 3-9 shows the contents of the FlyoutHelper class, which defines the static ShowRelativeToAppBar method and which I added in the Flyouts folder. This method takes care of positioning the Popup correctly relative to an AppBar button, but to do this, it needs to the Popup control, the Page that contains the AppBar, the AppBar control, and the Button that was clicked. This isn't ideal, but it is the only way I have found to reliably position a flyout.

Listing 3-9. Positioning a Popup Control Relative to an AppBar Button

```
using System;
using Windows.Foundation;
using Windows.UI.Xaml;
```

```
using Windows.UI.Xaml.Controls;
using Windows.UI.Xaml.Controls.Primitives;

namespace GrocerApp.Flyouts {
    class FlyoutHelper {

        public static void ShowRelativeToAppBar(Popup popup, Page page,
            AppBar appbar, Button button) {

            Func<UIElement, UIElement, Point> getOffset =
                delegate(UIElement control1, UIElement control2) {
                    return control1.TransformToVisual(control2)
                        .TransformPoint(new Point(0, 0));
                };

            Point popupOffset = getOffset(popup, page);

            Point buttonOffset = getOffset(button, page);
            popup.HorizontalOffset = buttonOffset.X - popupOffset.X
                - (popup.ActualWidth / 2) + (button.ActualWidth / 2);
            popup.VerticalOffset = getOffset(appbar, page).Y
                - popupOffset.Y - popup.ActualHeight;

            if (popupOffset.X + popup.HorizontalOffset
                + popup.ActualWidth > page.ActualWidth) {

                popup.HorizontalOffset = page.ActualWidth
                    - popupOffset.X - popup.ActualWidth;
            } else if (popup.HorizontalOffset + popupOffset.X < 0) {
                popup.HorizontalOffset = -popupOffset.X;
            }
        }

    }
}
```

The code positions the Popup just above the AppBar button that it relates to and is repositioned if that would mean that the Popup would disappear off the left or right edge of the screen. I am not going into the details of this code because it is convoluted. Instead, I recommend you use this code verbatim and dig into it only if you have problems. If you do have problems, the most likely cause will be that you have not set the Width and Height attributes for the Popup.

Showing and Hiding the Popup Control

The other function that my HomeZipCodeFlyout class is responsible for is showing and hiding the Popup. There is some sleight of hand in the way that my flyout works, which I use to simplify this code. If you look back at the XAML in Listing 3-6, you will see that I have specified a Mode for my data binding, like this:

```
...
<TextBox Height="40" Width="150" Text="{Binding Path=HomeZipCode,
    Mode=TwoWay}" />
...
```

Data bindings are one-way by default, meaning that changes in the view model update the control. I have specified a two-way binding, which means that, in addition, the value that the user enters into the TextBox control will be used to update the corresponding view model property.

▮ **Tip** Notice that I don't have to set the DataContext to make the binding work. The user control will be added to the main XAML layout, which means that it inherits the value of the DataContext from the top-level Page object.

This allows me to deal with the OK button being clicked by simply hiding the Popup; I don't have to worry about getting the value from the TextBox and explicitly updating the view model. The downside of this approach is that the view model may be updated multiple times before the flyout is dismissed, which can cause problems if you are listening for changes to the affected property elsewhere in your app. This isn't an issue for the HomeZipCode property, and I wanted to show you this technique, which can be a very neat way of dealing with user input.

Adding the Flyout to the App

The reason I have gone to the trouble of creating a user control is because I want to keep the XAML for my main layout as focused as possible. I still have to add the user control to the XAML, however. You can see how I have done this in Listing 3-10, which shows the changes I have made to the ListPage.xaml file.

Listing 3-10. Adding a Flyout Control to the ListPage XAML

```
<Page
    x:Class="GrocerApp.Pages.ListPage"
    xmlns="http://schemas.microsoft.com/winfx/2006/xaml/presentation"
    xmlns:x="http://schemas.microsoft.com/winfx/2006/xaml"
    xmlns:local="using:GrocerApp.Pages"
    xmlns:flyouts="using:GrocerApp.Flyouts"
    xmlns:d="http://schemas.microsoft.com/expression/blend/2008"
    xmlns:mc="http://schemas.openxmlformats.org/markup-compatibility/2006"
    mc:Ignorable="d">
```

```
<Grid Background="{StaticResource AppBackgroundColor}">

    <Grid.RowDefinitions>
        <RowDefinition/>
        <RowDefinition/>
    </Grid.RowDefinitions>
    <Grid.ColumnDefinitions>
        <ColumnDefinition/>
        <ColumnDefinition/>
    </Grid.ColumnDefinitions>

    <StackPanel Grid.RowSpan="2">
        // ...contents removed for brevity
    </StackPanel>

    <StackPanel Orientation="Vertical" Grid.Column="1">
        // ...contents removed for brevity
    </StackPanel>

    <StackPanel Orientation="Vertical" Grid.Column="1" Grid.Row="1">
        // ...contents removed for brevity
    </StackPanel>

    <flyouts:HomeZipCodeFlyout x:Name="HomeZipFlyout"/>
</Grid>

<Page.BottomAppBar>
    // ...contents removed for brevity
</Page.BottomAppBar>
</Page>
```

I have to define a new XAML namespace so that I can use the user control in the Flyouts folder, so I have added the following line to the XAML:

```
xmlns:flyouts="using: GrocerApp.Flyouts"
```

The important part is the name that I assign after the xmlns part, which is flyouts in this case. I have to use the same name when I declare my user control, like this:

```
<flyouts:HomeZipCodeFlyout x:Name="HomeZipFlyout"/>
```

Notice that the declaration for the flyout goes *inside* the Grid; even though it is not immediately displayed, the flyout user control must be declared as part of the main app layout, and Page controls can have only regular child elements (which is why the AppBar control has to be declared inside the Page.BottomAppBar property).

Showing the Flyout

All that remains is to hook up my flyout so it is displayed when the user clicks the AppBar button. Listing 3-11 shows the addition to the ListPage.xaml.cs file that makes this happen.

Listing 3-11. Showing the Flyout in Response to the AppBar Button Being Clicked

```
...
private void AppBarButtonClick(object sender, RoutedEventArgs e) {
    if (e.OriginalSource == AppBarDoneButton
            && viewModel.SelectedItemIndex > -1) {

        viewModel.GroceryList.RemoveAt(viewModel.SelectedItemIndex);
        viewModel.SelectedItemIndex = -1;

    } else if (e.OriginalSource == AppBarZipButton) {
        HomeZipFlyout.Show(this, this.BottomAppBar, (Button)e.OriginalSource);
    }
}
...
```

I call the Show method I defined in my user control, passing in the set of controls that I need to correctly position the Popup. You can see the result in Figure 3-2.

Figure 3-2. Displaying a flyout next to the AppBar button it relates to

Creating a More Complex Flyout

Now that I have demonstrated the basics, I can build a flyout that will allow the user to add new items to the grocery list. The difference in this flyout is that it won't be able to rely on the two-way binding trick for dealing with the view model. This isn't an especially complex technique; I just want to show you both approaches so you can pick the one that works for your projects. The more flyout examples I can show you, the easier you will find it when you come to create your own.

To start, I used the UserControl template to create the AddItemFlyout.xaml file in the Flyouts project folder. I then followed the same basic approach of laying out my content in a Popup, as shown in Listing 3-12.

Listing 3-12. The XAML for the AddItem Flyout

```
<UserControl
    x:Class="GrocerApp.Flyouts.AddItemFlyout"
    xmlns="http://schemas.microsoft.com/winfx/2006/xaml/presentation"
    xmlns:x="http://schemas.microsoft.com/winfx/2006/xaml"
    xmlns:local="using:GrocerApp.Flyouts"
    xmlns:d="http://schemas.microsoft.com/expression/blend/2008"
    xmlns:mc="http://schemas.openxmlformats.org/markup-compatibility/2006"
    mc:Ignorable="d"
    d:DesignHeight="300"
    d:DesignWidth="400">

    <Popup x:Name="AddItemPopup" IsLightDismissEnabled="True" Width="435"
    Height="265" >
        <StackPanel Background="Black">
            <Border Background="#85C54C" BorderThickness="4">
                <Grid Margin="10">
                    <Grid.RowDefinitions>
                        <RowDefinition/>
                        <RowDefinition/>
                        <RowDefinition/>
                        <RowDefinition/>
                    </Grid.RowDefinitions>
                    <Grid.ColumnDefinitions>
                        <ColumnDefinition Width="Auto"/>
                        <ColumnDefinition Width="300"/>
                    </Grid.ColumnDefinitions>

                    <TextBlock Text="Name:" Style="{StaticResource
                            AddItemText}"  />
                    <TextBlock Text="Quantity:" Grid.Row="1"
                            Style="{StaticResource AddItemText}" />
                    <TextBlock Text="Store:" Grid.Row="2"
                            Style="{StaticResource AddItemText}" />

                    <TextBox x:Name="ItemName" Grid.Column="1"
                            Style="{StaticResource AddItemTextBox}" />
                    <TextBox x:Name="ItemQuantity" Grid.Row="1" Grid.
                            Column="1"
                            Style="{StaticResource AddItemTextBox}" />
                    <ComboBox x:Name="ItemStore" Grid.Column="1" Grid.
                            Row="2"
```

```
                      Style="{StaticResource AddItemStore}"
                      ItemsSource="{Binding StoreList}"
                      DisplayMemberPath="" />
            <StackPanel Orientation="Horizontal" Grid.Row="3"
                      HorizontalAlignment="Center"
                      Grid.ColumnSpan="2">
                <Button Click="AddButtonClick">Add Item</Button>
            </StackPanel>
          </Grid>
        </Border>
      </StackPanel>
    </Popup>
</UserControl>
```

The layout of the Popup is very similar to the layout of the ItemDetail page that I created in Chapter 2. It is possible to embed Frame controls (and therefore Pages) into Popups for flyouts, but the effort required to adjust the styling and change the code-behind behavior often makes it more attractive to simply duplicate the elements. I am happy to do this for simple projects, even though I have a nagging feeling that I will be revisiting the project at some point to remove the duplication and do it properly.

Writing the Code

The part of this flyout that I want you to see is in the code, which is shown in Listing 3-13.

Listing 3-13. The AddItemFlyout.xaml.cs File

```
using System;
using GrocerApp.Data;
using Windows.UI.Xaml;
using Windows.UI.Xaml.Controls;

namespace GrocerApp.Flyouts {
    public sealed partial class AddItemFlyout : UserControl {

        public AddItemFlyout() {
            this.InitializeComponent();
        }

        public void Show(Page page, AppBar appbar, Button button) {
            AddItemPopup.IsOpen = true;
            FlyoutHelper.ShowRelativeToAppBar(AddItemPopup, page, appbar,
            button);
        }

        private void AddButtonClick(object sender, RoutedEventArgs e) {
```

```
((ViewModel)DataContext).GroceryList.Add(new GroceryItem {
    Name = ItemName.Text,
    Quantity = Int32.Parse(ItemQuantity.Text),
    Store = ItemStore.SelectedItem.ToString()
});

        AddItemPopup.IsOpen = false;
    }
  }
}
```

I need to get my view model object so I can add the new item to it. There are several ways of doing this, but the simplest is to read the value of the DataContext property, as shown in the listing. Some care is required, because I am making the assumption that the value of this property will be my ViewModel object, which I set in the constructor of the ListPage class (in the ListPage.xaml.cs file). As I mentioned at the time, the DataContext property is inherited, which means that the object I set for the Page object can be retrieved from my UserControl, but only if another object hasn't been assigned to the DataContext property of one of the intermediate controls in the layout hierarchy.

Once I have the ViewModel object, it is a simple matter to add a new GroceryItem to the GroceryList collection. Since the collection is observable, the addition will automatically be reflected in the rest of the app.

Adding the Flyout to the App

All that remains is to add my new flyout to the ListPage layout and code, which I do following the same pattern as for the previous flyout. Listing 3-14 shows the XAML declaration for the flyout.

Listing 3-14. Declaring the Add Item Flyout in the XAML

```
...
<flyouts:HomeZipCodeFlyout x:Name="HomeZipFlyout"/>
<flyouts:AddItemFlyout x:Name="AddItemFlyout"/>
...
```

Listing 3-15 shows the addition to the AppBarButtonClick in the ListPage class, which shows the flyout in response to the Add Item AppBar button being clicked.

Listing 3-15. Showing the Flyout in Response to the AppBar Button

```
...
private void AppBarButtonClick(object sender, RoutedEventArgs e) {
    if (e.OriginalSource == AppBarDoneButton
            && viewModel.SelectedItemIndex > -1) {

        viewModel.GroceryList.RemoveAt(viewModel.SelectedItemIndex);
        viewModel.SelectedItemIndex = -1;
```

```
    } else if (e.OriginalSource == AppBarZipButton) {
        HomeZipFlyout.Show(this, this.BottomAppBar, (Button)
        e.OriginalSource);
    } else if (e.OriginalSource == AppBarAddButton) {
        AddItemFlyout.Show(this, this.BottomAppBar, (Button)
        e.OriginalSource);
    }
}
...
```

You can see how the flyout appears in Figure 3-3. The "light dismiss" style for flyout Popup controls associated with the AppBar means that only one flyout will be shown at a time.

Figure 3-3. *The Add Item flyout*

Navigating Within a Windows App

If your app contains distinct functionality sections, then you need to provide a Navigation Bar (NavBar) so that the user can easily move between them. The simplest way to provide consistent navigation is to restructure the app so that the functional areas are presented in a Frame control within a wrapper page.

Creating the Wrapper

I created the MainPage.xaml file in the Pages folder to act as my wrapper. You can see the content of this file, which I created using the Blank Page template, in Listing 3-16.

Listing 3-16. The MainPage.xaml File

```
<Page
    x:Class="GrocerApp.Pages.MainPage"
    xmlns="http://schemas.microsoft.com/winfx/2006/xaml/presentation"
    xmlns:x="http://schemas.microsoft.com/winfx/2006/xaml"
    xmlns:local="using:GrocerApp.Pages"
    xmlns:d="http://schemas.microsoft.com/expression/blend/2008"
    xmlns:mc="http://schemas.openxmlformats.org/markup-compatibility/2006"
    mc:Ignorable="d">

    <Page.TopAppBar>
        <AppBar>
            <StackPanel Orientation="Horizontal"
            HorizontalAlignment="Center">
                <Button x:Name="ListViewButton"
                    Style="{StaticResource AppBarButtonStyle}"
                    AutomationProperties.Name="List View"
                    Content="&#xE14C;" Click="NavBarButtonPress"/>

                <Button x:Name="DetailViewButton"
                    Style="{StaticResource AppBarButtonStyle}"
                    AutomationProperties.Name="Detail View"
                    Content="&#xE1A3;" Click="NavBarButtonPress"/>
            </StackPanel>
        </AppBar>
    </Page.TopAppBar>

    <Grid Background="{StaticResource ApplicationPageBackgroundThemeBrush}">
        <Frame x:Name="MainFrame" />
    </Grid>
</Page>
```

To add a NavBar, I declare an `AppBar` control within the `Page.TopAppBar` property. The mechanics of the NavBar are the same as the (bottom) AppBar, and I have added two `Button` controls to support navigation between the two views that the app contains.

In addition to the NavBar, the layout of the `MainPage` contains a `Frame`, which I will use to display the different views.

The code to support this layout is very simple and is shown in Listing 3-17. I respond to either of the `Button` controls being clicked by navigating to the appropriate `Page` and changing the `IsChecked` property of the buttons. I have also created the `ViewModel` object in this class so that there is just one instance across the entire app. The object is passed to the individual pages through the `Frame.Navigate` method.

Listing 3-17. The MainPage.xaml.cs

```
using System;
using GrocerApp.Data;
using Windows.UI.Xaml;
using Windows.UI.Xaml.Controls;
using Windows.UI.Xaml.Controls.Primitives;
using Windows.UI.Xaml.Navigation;

namespace GrocerApp.Pages {

    public sealed partial class MainPage : Page {
        private ViewModel viewModel;

        public MainPage() {
            this.InitializeComponent();

            viewModel = new ViewModel();

            viewModel.StoreList.Add("Whole Foods");
            vicwModel.StoreList.Add("Kroger");
            viewModel.StoreList.Add("Costco");
            viewModel.StoreList.Add("Walmart");

            viewModel.GroceryList.Add(new GroceryItem {
                Name = "Apples",
                Quantity = 4, Store - "Whole Foods"
            });
            viewModel.GroceryList.Add(new GroceryItem {
                Name = "Hotdogs",
                Quantity = 12, Store = "Costco"
            });
            viewModel.GroceryList.Add(new GroceryItem {
                Name = "Soda",
                Quantity = 2, Store = "Costco"
            });
            viewModel.GroceryList.Add(new GroceryItem {
                Name = "Eggs",
                Quantity = 12, Store = "Kroger"
            });

            this.DataContext = viewModel;

            MainFrame.Navigate(typeof(ListPage), viewModel);
        }

        protected override void OnNavigatedTo(NavigationEventArgs e) {
        }
```

```
        private void NavBarButtonPress(object sender, RoutedEventArgs e) {
            Boolean isListView = (Button)sender == ListViewButton;
            MainFrame.Navigate(isListView ? typeof(ListPage)
                : typeof(DetailPage), viewModel);
        }
    }
}
```

I navigate to the default view for my app in the constructor, which is the `ListPage` I have been using in earlier examples.

■ **Tip**   The `ListPage` has been refactored so that the view model is obtained from the arguments to the `OnNavigatedTo` method. I am not going to list those changes here because they are so simple, but you can see the modified class in the source code download that accompanies this book and that is available from Apress.com.

I have to update the `App.xaml.cs` file to put my wrapper view into place, as shown in Listing 3-18.

Listing 3-18. Making MainPage the Default Page for the Example App

```
...
if (rootFrame.Content == null) {

    if (!rootFrame.Navigate(typeof(Pages.MainPage), args.Arguments)) {
        throw new Exception("Failed to create initial page");
    }
}
...
```

Creating the Other View

I need to add another page to the application using the `Blank  Page` template . I have created a placeholder called `DetailPage.xaml` in the `Pages` project folder; the layout is shown in Listing 3-19.

Listing 3-19. The DetailPage.xaml File

```
<Page
    x:Class="GrocerApp.Pages.DetailPage"
    xmlns="http://schemas.microsoft.com/winfx/2006/xaml/presentation"
    xmlns:x="http://schemas.microsoft.com/winfx/2006/xaml"
    xmlns:local="using:GrocerApp.Pages"
    xmlns:d="http://schemas.microsoft.com/expression/blend/2008"
```

```
xmlns:mc="http://schemas.openxmlformats.org/markup-compatibility/2006"
mc:Ignorable="d">

<Grid Background="{StaticResource ApplicationPageBackgroundThemeBrush}">
    <StackPanel VerticalAlignment="Center" HorizontalAlignment="Center">
        <TextBlock Style="{StaticResource HeaderTextStyle}" Text="Detail
            View"/>
    </StackPanel>
</Grid>
</Page>
```

This page doesn't contain any functionality; it just exists so that I can show you how to handle navigation within an app.

Testing the Navigation

All that remains is to test the navigation. If you start the example app and bring up the AppBar, you will see that the NavBar appears automatically as well, as shown in Figure 3-4.

Figure 3-4. *The NavBar shown with the page-specific AppBar*

Click the Detail View button in the NavBar, and you'll see the alternative view, as shown in Figure 3-5.

Figure 3-5. *Displaying the other content view in the app*

This is a nice feature where the page-specific AppBars are seamlessly integrated with the app-wide navigation controls. You can implement a single AppBar for the app by declaring it in the wrapper page. If you do this, you become responsible for ensuring that buttons are added and removed from the AppBar as needed.

Summary

In this chapter, I showed you how to create AppBars, NavBars, and flyouts, which, between them, provide essential parts of the Windows 8 app user experience. Implementing these interactions is important in making your app consistent with the broader user experience, and I recommend you take the time to ensure that the controls you display are always relevant to the content and view the user is presented with. In the next chapter, I'll show you some features that allow your app to integrate into Windows: *tiles* and *badges*.

CHAPTER 4

■ ■ ■

Views and Tiles

In this chapter, I describe two of the features that allow an app to fit into the wider user experience presented by Windows 8. The first of these features is the way that apps can be *snapped* and *filled* so that two apps can be viewed side by side. I show you how to adapt when your app is placed into one of these layouts and how to change the layout when your interactions don't fit inside the view constraints.

The second feature is the *tile* model. Tiles are at the heart of the Windows 8 replacement for the Start menu. At their simplest, they are static buttons that can be used to launch your app, but with a little work, they can present the user with an invaluable snapshot of the state of your app, allowing the user to get an overview without having to run the app itself. In this chapter, I show you how to create dynamic tiles by applying updates and by using a related feature, *badges*. Table 4-1 provides the summary for this chapter.

Table 4-1. *Chapter Summary*

Problem	Solution	Listing
Adapt an app's layout when it has been placed into a snapped or filled view.	Handle the ViewStateChanged event by modifying the layout of your controls.	1–3
Declare the adaptions required for view changes using XAML.	Use the VisualStateManage.	4, 5
Break out of the snapped view.	Use the TryUnsnap method.	6, 7
Create a live tile for an app.	Modify the content of an XML template and use the classes in the Windows.UI.Notification namespace.	8–10
Update square and wide tiles.	Prepare updates for two templates and merge them together.	11, 12
Apply a badge to a tile	Populate and apply an XML badge template	13, 14

Supporting Views

So far, my app has assumed that it has full and exclusive use of the display screen. However, apps can be arranged by the number so that they are *snapped* or *filled*. A snapped app occupies a 320-pixel strip at the left or right edge of the screen. A filled app is displayed alongside a snapped app and occupies the entire screen except for the 320-pixel strip. To demonstrate the different views, I have added some content to the DetailPage.xaml file, as shown in Listing 4-1. (This is the file I added in the previous chapter to demonstrate navigation, but it didn't contain any functionality other than a simple message.)

Listing 4-1. Adding Content to the DetailPage.xaml File

```
<Page
    x:Class="GrocerApp.Pages.DetailPage"
    xmlns="http://schemas.microsoft.com/winfx/2006/xaml/presentation"
    xmlns:x="http://schemas.microsoft.com/winfx/2006/xaml"
    xmlns:local="using:GrocerApp.Pages"
    xmlns:d="http://schemas.microsoft.com/expression/blend/2008"
    xmlns:mc="http://schemas.openxmlformats.org/markup-compatibility/2006"
    mc:Ignorable="d">

    <Grid x:Name="GridLayout" Background="#71C524">
        <Grid.RowDefinitions>
            <RowDefinition/>
            <RowDefinition/>
        </Grid.RowDefinitions>
        <Grid.ColumnDefinitions>
            <ColumnDefinition/>
            <ColumnDefinition/>
        </Grid.ColumnDefinitions>

        <StackPanel x:Name="TopLeft" Background="#3E790A">
            <TextBlock x:Name="TopLeftText"
                    Style="{StaticResource DetailViewLabelStyle}"
                    Text="Top-Left"/>
        </StackPanel>

        <StackPanel x:Name="TopRight" Background="#70a524" Grid.Column="1"
                    Grid.Row="0">
            <TextBlock x:Name="TopRightText"
                    Style="{StaticResource DetailViewLabelStyle}"
                    Text="Top-Right"/>
        </StackPanel>
```

```
        <StackPanel x:Name="BottomLeft" Background="#1E3905" Grid.Row="1">
            <TextBlock x:Name="BottomLeftText"
                        Style="{StaticResource DetailViewLabelStyle}"
                        Text="Bottom-Left"/>
        </StackPanel>

        <StackPanel x:Name="BottomRight" Background="#45860B" Grid.
                    Column="1" Grid.Row="1">
            <TextBlock x:Name="BottomRightText"
                        Style="{StaticResource DetailViewLabelStyle}"
                        Text="Bottom-Right"/>
        </StackPanel>
    </Grid>
</Page>
```

I have defined a new style called DetailViewLabelStyle for this page in the /Resources/GrocerResourceDictionary.xaml file, as shown in Listing 4-2.

Listing 4-2. Adding the DetailViewLabelStyle Style

```
...
<Style x:Key="DetailViewLabelStyle" TargetType="TextBlock"
        BasedOn="{StaticResource HeaderTextStyle}">
    <Setter Property="FontSize" Value="50"/>
    <Setter Property="Margin" Value="10"/>
    <Setter Property="HorizontalAlignment" Value="Left"/>
</Style>
...
```

This layout creates a simple colored grid. You can see this new content by starting the app and using the NavBar I added in the previous chapter to navigate using the Detail View button.

Figure 4-1 shows the app in its filled and snapped views. The remaining space is a simple app that reports its view. I use this for testing and have included it in the source code download for this book, which you can get from Apress.com.

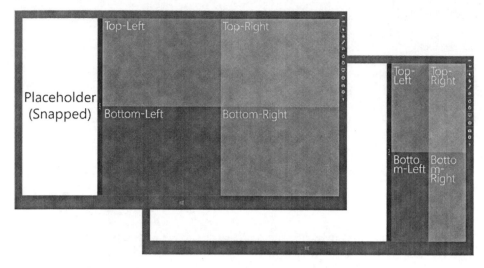

Figure 4-1. *The example app shown in the filled and snapped views*

■ **Note** Apps can be snapped only in the landscape view, and Windows 8 supports snapping only if the horizontal resolution of the display is 1366 pixels or greater. You must ensure that you have selected the correct orientation and resolution in the simulator if you want to experiment with snapping.

The loss of 320 pixels to make room for the snapped app doesn't cause a lot of disruption for most apps. The problems start to appear when your app is moved from the filled to the snapped view, which you can see on the right of the figure. Clearly, the app needs to adapt to the new view, and in the sections that follow, I'll show you the different mechanisms available for doing just that.

■ **Tip** You can move through the different views for an app by pressing Win+. (the Windows and period keys). Each time you press these keys, the app will cycle into a new view.

Responding to View Changes in Code

You monitor changes in the view through the Page.SizeChanged event. By handling this event, you can determine the current view through the Windows.UI.ViewManagement. ApplicationView.Value property and reconfigure your app as required. Listing 4-3 shows the code for the DetailPagepage, with additions to handle this event.

Listing 4-3. Controlling the View in the DetailPage Code-Behind Class

```
using Windows.UI.ViewManagement;
using Windows.UI.Xaml;
using Windows.UI.Xaml.Controls;
using Windows.UI.Xaml.Navigation;

namespace GrocerApp.Pages {
    public sealed partial class DetailPage : Page {

        public DetailPage() {
            this.InitializeComponent();

            SizeChanged += DetailPage_SizeChanged;
        }

        void DetailPage_SizeChanged(object sender, SizeChangedEventArgs e) {
            if (ApplicationView.Value == ApplicationViewState.Snapped) {
                GridLayout.ColumnDefinitions[0].Width
                    = new GridLength(0);
            } else {
                GridLayout.ColumnDefinitions[0].Width
                    = new GridLength(1, GridUnitType.Star);
            }
        }

        protected override void OnNavigatedTo(NavigationEventArgs e) {
        }
    }
}
```

The ApplicationView.View property returns a value from the ApplicationViewState enumeration, describing the current view. The values in this enumeration are Snapped, Filled, FullScreenPortrait, and FullScreenLandscape; these last two allow you to differentiate between the landscape and portrait modes when the app is shown full-screen.

In my example, the DetailPage_SizeChanged method determines the kind of view being used and adapts the app layout accordingly. If the app is being shown in the snapped view, then I set the width of the first column in my grid to zero. Your app state isn't reset automatically when the app is restored to the full-screen view, so you must also define code to handle the other event states. In this case, for any other view but snapped, I reset the width of the column. (The syntax for working with columns is awkward, but you get the idea.) You can see the change in the snapped view in Figure 4-2.

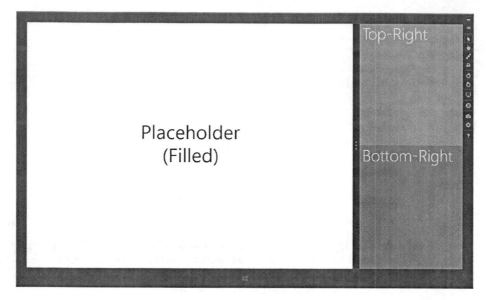

Figure 4-2. Adapting to the restrictions of the snapped view

Rather than squishing everything into a tiny window, I have shown only part of my app. Showing reduced functionality is the most sensible way of dealing with the relatively small amount of screen space that a snapped app has access to. You will be surprised just how much you can pack into this space, but it just isn't the same as having access to the full screen.

Responding to View Changes in XAML

You can set out the changes you want to make to your app using XAML. The XAML syntax for this is verbose, hard to read, and more difficult to work with—so much so that I recommend you stick with the code approach. But for completeness, Listing 4-4 shows how I can specify the changes I want using XAML.

■ **Note**   The VisualStateManager feature, which is what this XAML uses, is a standard WPF and Silverlight feature. It has a lot of features, and I am unable to give it full attention in this book. My advice is to use the code-based approach, but if you are a true XAML fan, then you can see the WPF or Silverlight documentation for further details of the elements you can use.

Listing 4-4. Defining View Changes in XAML

```xaml
<Page
    x:Class="GrocerApp.Pages.DetailPage"
    xmlns="http://schemas.microsoft.com/winfx/2006/xaml/presentation"
    xmlns:x="http://schemas.microsoft.com/winfx/2006/xaml"
    xmlns:local="using:GrocerApp.Pages"
    xmlns:d="http://schemas.microsoft.com/expression/blend/2008"
    xmlns:mc="http://schemas.openxmlformats.org/markup-compatibility/2006"
    mc:Ignorable="d">

<Grid x:Name="GridLayout" Background="#71C524">

    <VisualStateManager.VisualStateGroups>
        <VisualStateGroup x:Name="OrientationStates">
            <VisualState x:Name="Snapped">
                <Storyboard>
                    <ObjectAnimationUsingKeyFrames
                            Storyboard.TargetProperty="Grid.
                            ColumnDefinitions[0].Width"
                            Storyboard.TargetName="GridLayout">
                        <DiscreteObjectKeyFrame KeyTime="0">
                            <DiscreteObjectKeyFrame.Value>
                                <GridLength>0</GridLength>
                            </DiscreteObjectKeyFrame.Value>
                        </DiscreteObjectKeyFrame>
                    </ObjectAnimationUsingKeyFrames>
                </Storyboard>
            </VisualState>

            <VisualState x:Name="Others">
                <Storyboard>
                    <ObjectAnimationUsingKeyFrames
                            Storyboard.TargetProperty="Grid.
                            ColumnDefinitions[0].Width"
                            Storyboard.TargetName="GridLayout">
                        <DiscreteObjectKeyFrame KeyTime="0">
                            <DiscreteObjectKeyFrame.Value>
                                <GridLength>*</GridLength>
                            </DiscreteObjectKeyFrame.Value>
                        </DiscreteObjectKeyFrame>
                    </ObjectAnimationUsingKeyFrames>
                </Storyboard>
            </VisualState>

        </VisualStateGroup>
    </VisualStateManager.VisualStateGroups>
```

```
    <Grid.RowDefinitions>
        <RowDefinition/>
        <RowDefinition/>
    </Grid.RowDefinitions>
    <Grid.ColumnDefinitions>
        <ColumnDefinition/>
        <ColumnDefinition/>
    </Grid.ColumnDefinitions>

    // ...StackPanel elements removed for brevity...
</Grid>
</Page>
```

In this listing, I have declared two VisualState elements. The first, Snapped, sets the width of the first column to zero pixels. This is the state I will enter when the app is snapped. The second is called Others, and it restores the width. This is the state that I will enter when the app is not snapped. You can see what I mean about verbosity; it takes me 31 lines of XAML to replace 8 lines of code.

And, I still have to handle the SizeChanged event so that I can enter the XAML states I defined. Listing 4-5 shows the changes required to the code-behind file.

Listing 4-5. Invoking the VisualStateManager in Response to the ViewStateChanged Event

```
using Windows.UI.ViewManagement;
using Windows.UI.Xaml;
using Windows.UI.Xaml.Controls;
using Windows.UI.Xaml.Navigation;

namespace GrocerApp.Pages {
    public sealed partial class DetailPage : Page {

        public DetailPage() {
            this.InitializeComponent();
            SizeChanged += DetailPage_SizeChanged;
        }

        void DetailPage_SizeChanged(object sender, SizeChangedEventArgs e) {
            //if (ApplicationView.Value == ApplicationViewState.Snapped) {
            //    GridLayout.ColumnDefinitions[0].Width
            //        = new GridLength(0);
            //} else {
            //    GridLayout.ColumnDefinitions[0].Width
            //        = new GridLength(1, GridUnitType.Star);
            //}

            string stateName = ApplicationView.Value ==
                ApplicationViewState.Snapped ? "Snapped" : "Others";
            VisualStateManager.GoToState(this, stateName, false);
        }
```

```
    protected override void OnNavigatedTo(NavigationEventArgs e) {
    }
  }
}
```

I call the static `VisualStateManager.GoToState` method to move between the states I defined in XAML. The arguments for this method are the current `Page` object, the name of the state to enter, and whether intermediate states should be displayed. This last argument should be true, since Windows provides the animations for transition between views.

Breaking Out of the Snapped View

If you are presenting the user with reduced functionality in the snapped view, you may to revert to a wider view when the user interacts with your app in certain ways. To demonstrate this, I have added a `Button` to the layout for the `DetailPage` page, as shown in Listing 4-6.

Listing 4-6. Adding a Button to the Layout

```
. . .
<StackPanel x:Name="TopRight" Background="#70a524" Grid.Column="1"
    Grid.Row="0">
    <TextBlock x:Name="TopRightText"
               Style="{StaticResource DetailViewLabelStyle}"
               Text="Top-Right"/>
    <Button Click="HandleButtonClick">Unsnap</Button>
</StackPanel>
. . .
```

Listing 4-7 shows the handler for the `Click` event, which unsnaps the app using the `TryUnsnap` method.

Listing 4-7. Unsnapping an App

```
using Windows.UI.ViewManagement;
using Windows.UI.Xaml;
using Windows.UI.Xaml.Controls;
using Windows.UI.Xaml.Navigation;

namespace GrocerApp.Pages {
    public sealed partial class DetailPage : Page {

        public DetailPage() {
            this.InitializeComponent();

            SizeChanged += DetailPage_SizeChanged;
        }
```

```
        void DetailPage_SizeChanged(object sender, SizeChangedEventArgs e) {
            //if (ApplicationView.Value == ApplicationViewState.Snapped) {
            //    GridLayout.ColumnDefinitions[0].Width
            //        = new GridLength(0);
            //} else {
            //    GridLayout.ColumnDefinitions[0].Width
            //        = new GridLength(1, GridUnitType.Star);
            //}

            string stateName = ApplicationView.Value ==
                ApplicationViewState.Snapped ? "Snapped" : "Others";
            VisualStateManager.GoToState(this, stateName, false);

        }

        private void HandleButtonClick(object sender, RoutedEventArgs e) {
            Windows.UI.ViewManagement.ApplicationView.TryUnsnap();
        }

        protected override void OnNavigatedTo(NavigationEventArgs e) {
        }
    }
}
```

The TryUnsnap method will change the view, but only in response to user interaction. You can't change the view if the app is in the background, for example.

Using Tiles and Badges

Tiles are the representation of your app on the Start screen. At their simplest, tiles are static icons for starting your app. However, with a little effort, you can use your tile to present the user with a useful summary of your app's state and to draw their attention to activities they may want to perform.

In the sections that follow, I demonstrate how to present information through the tile of my example app. There are two possible, and conflicting, goals when you create a dynamic tile; you are either trying to encourage the user to run your app or dissuading them from running it. If you are trying to attract the user, then your tile becomes an advert for the experience, insights, or content that you offer. This is appropriate for entertainment apps or those that present external content such as news.

Dissuading the user from running an app may seem like a strange goal, but it can significantly improve the user experience. Consider productivity apps as an example. I dread to think of the hours I have lost waiting for calendar or to-do apps to load just so I can check where my next appointment is or what my most urgent actions requires. You can reduce the friction and frustration that your users experience when using your app and create a more pleasing and immediate experience by displaying the information that the user needs in your app tile.

Both goals require careful thought. The overall Windows 8 experience is flat, simple, and subdued. If you are using your tile as an ad, then the muted nature of Windows makes it easy to create tiles that stand out. If you go too far, though, you will create something that is discordant and jarring and is more of an eyesore than an attraction.

If your goal is to reduce the number of times the user needs to run your app, then you need to present the right information at the right time. This requires a good understanding of what drives your users to adopt your app and the ability to customize the data that is presented. Adaptability is essential; there is no point showing me the most urgent work action on my task list on a Saturday morning, for example. Every time you present the user with the wrong information, you force them to run your app to get what they do need.

■ **Tip** An app can update its tile only when it is running. In Chapter 5, I detail the app life cycle, and you will learn that apps are put into a suspended state when the user switches to another app. This means you can't provide updates in the background. Windows 8 supports a push model where you can send XML updates from the cloud, but this requires setting up server infrastructure to support your app.

Improving Static Tiles

The simplest way to improve the appearance of your app in the Start screen is to change the images used for your app's tile. You should customize the images for your app, even if you don't use any other tile features.

To do this, you will need a set of three images of specific sizes: 30 by 30 pixels, 150 by 150 pixels, and 310 by 150 pixels. These images should contain the logo or text you want to display but be otherwise transparent. I used a barcode motif for my example app, creating images called tile30.png, tile150.png, and tile310.png and placing them in the Assets folder of my Visual Studio project.

To apply the new images, open the Package.appxmanifest file from the Solution Explorer. There is a Tile section on Application UI tab that has options to set the logo, wide logo, and small logo. There are hints to explain which size is required for each option. You will also have to set the background color that will be used for the tile; I set mine to the same color I use for the background of my app (the hex RGB value #3E790A), as shown in Figure 4-3.

Tile:		
Logo:	Assets\tile150.png	× [...]
	Required size: 150 x 150 pixels	
Wide logo:	Assets\tile310.png	× [...]
	Required size: 310 x 150 pixels	
Small logo:	Assets\tile30.png	× [...]
	Required size: 30 x 30 pixels	
Short name:		
Show name:	All Logos ▾	
Foreground text:	Light ▾	
Background color:	#3E790A	

Figure 4-3. *Applying images in the app manifest*

■ **Tip**   It is important to set the background color in the manifest, rather than include a background in the images. When you update a tile, which I demonstrate in the next section, the image is replaced with dynamic information on a backdrop of the color specified in the manifest.

You may have to uninstall your app from the start screen for the tile images to take effect. The next time you start your app from Visual Studio, you should see the new static tile; you can toggle between the standard and wide views by selecting the tile, right-clicking, and picking the Larger or Smaller buttons from the AppBar. You can see the square and wide tile formats for the example app in Figure 4-4.

Figure 4-4. *The updated static wide tile*

Notice that the word GrocerApp is displayed at the bottom of the tile. This text is specified as the value for the Short Name option in the Application UI tab. The All Logos option for Show Name means that it is applied to both the regular and wide tiles.

■ **Tip** You can also replace the splash screen that is shown to the user when the app is loading. There is a Splash Screen section at the bottom of the Application UI tab in which you can specify the image and the background color it should be displayed with. The image used for the splash screen must be 630 pixels by 300 pixels.

Creating Live Tiles

Live tiles provide information about your app to your user. For my example app, I am going to display the first few items from the grocery list. Tile updates are based on preconfigured templates, which contain a mix of graphics and text and which are designed for either standard or wide tiles. The first thing you must do is pick the template you want. The easiest way to do this is to look at the API documentation for the `Windows.UI.Notifications.TileTemplateType` enumeration, which is available at http://msdn.microsoft.com/en-us/library/windows/apps/windows.ui.notifications.tiletemplatetype.aspx. The template system is based on XML fragments, and you can see the XML structure for each template in the API documentation. I have chosen the `TileSquareText03` template. This is for a square tile and has four lines of nonwrapping text, without any images. You can see the XML fragment that represents the tile in Listing 4-8.

Listing 4-8. The XML Fragment for the TileSquareText03 Tile Template

```
<tile>
  <visual lang="en-US">
    <binding template="TileSquareText03">
      <text id="1">Text Field 1</text>
      <text id="2">Text Field 2</text>
      <text id="3">Text Field 3</text>
      <text id="4">Text Field 4</text>
    </binding>
  </visual>
</tile>
```

The idea is to populate the `text` elements with information from the app and pass the result to the Windows notifications system. I want to set up my tile updates in the `MainPage` class, but doing this means refactoring my app so that the `ViewModel` object is created there, rather than in the `ListPage` class. Listing 4-9 shows the changes required in the `MainPage` class to support the view model and to update the tiles.

Listing 4-9. Refactoring the MainPage Class

```
using GrocerApp.Data;
using System;
using Windows.Data.Xml.Dom;
using Windows.UI.Notifications;
using Windows.UI.Xaml;
```

```csharp
using Windows.UI.Xaml.Controls;
using Windows.UI.Xaml.Navigation;

namespace GrocerApp.Pages {

    public sealed partial class MainPage : Page {
        private ViewModel viewModel;

        public MainPage() {
            this.InitializeComponent();

            viewModel = new ViewModel();

            // ...test data removed for brevity...

            this.DataContext = viewModel;

            MainFrame.Navigate(typeof(ListPage), viewModel);

            viewModel.GroceryList.CollectionChanged += (sender, args) => {
                UpdateTile();
            };

            UpdateTile();
        }

        private void UpdateTile() {

            XmlDocument tileXml = TileUpdateManager.
                GetTemplateContent(TileTemplateType.TileSquareText03);

            XmlNodeList textNodes =
                tileXml.GetElementsByTagName("text");

            for (int i = 0; i < textNodes.Length &&
                    i < viewModel.GroceryList.Count; i++) {
                textNodes[i].InnerText = viewModel.GroceryList[i].Name;
            }

            for (int i = 0; i < 5; i++) {
                TileUpdateManager.CreateTileUpdaterForApplication()
                    .Update(new TileNotification(tileXml));
            }
        }
    }
```

```
protected override void OnNavigatedTo(NavigationEventArgs e) {
}

private void NavBarButtonPress(object sender, RoutedEventArgs e) {
    Boolean isListView = (Button)sender == ListViewButton;
    MainFrame.Navigate(isListView ? typeof(ListPage)
        : typeof(DetailPage), viewModel);

    }
  }
}
```

I also need to update the ListPage.xaml.cs file so that the view model object that is passed from the MainPage class is used, as shown in Listing 4-10.

Listing 4-10. Updating the ListPage Class in the ListPage.xaml.cs File

```
using GrocerApp.Data;
using Windows.UI.Xaml;
using Windows.UI.Xaml.Controls;
using Windows.UI.Xaml.Navigation;

namespace GrocerApp.Pages {

    public sealed partial class ListPage : Page {
        ViewModel viewModel;

        public ListPage() {
            this.InitializeComponent();
        }

        protected override void OnNavigatedTo(NavigationEventArgs e) {
            viewModel = (ViewModel)e.Parameter;

            ItemDetailFrame.Navigate(typeof(NoItemSelected));
            viewModel.PropertyChanged += (sender, args) => {
                if (args.PropertyName == "SelectedItemIndex") {
                    if (viewModel.SelectedItemIndex == -1) {
                        ItemDetailFrame.Navigate(typeof(NoItemSelected));
                        AppBarDoneButton.IsEnabled = false;
                    } else {
                        ItemDetailFrame.Navigate(typeof(ItemDetail),
                        viewModel);
                        AppBarDoneButton.IsEnabled = true;
                    }
                }
            };
        }
```

```
        private void ListSelectionChanged(object sender,
                SelectionChangedEventArgs e) {
            viewModel.SelectedItemIndex = groceryList.SelectedIndex;
        }

        private void AppBarButtonClick(object sender, RoutedEventArgs e) {
            if (e.OriginalSource == AppBarDoneButton
                    && viewModel.SelectedItemIndex > -1) {

                viewModel.GroceryList.RemoveAt(viewModel.SelectedItemIndex);
                viewModel.SelectedItemIndex = -1;

            } else if (e.OriginalSource == AppBarZipButton) {
                    HomeZipFlyout.Show(this, this.BottomAppBar,
                        (Button)e.OriginalSource);
            } else if (e.OriginalSource == AppBarAddButton) {
                AddItemFlyout.Show(this, this.BottomAppBar,
                    (Button)e.OriginalSource);
            }

        }
    }
}
```

There is a lot going on in just a few lines of code, so I'll break things down in the sections that follow

Populating the XML Template

To get the template XML fragment, I call the `TileUpdateManager.GetTemplateContent` method specifying the template I want with a value from the `TileTemplateType` enumeration. This gives me a `Windows.Data.Xml.Dom.XmlDocument` object to which I can apply standard DOM methods to set the value of the `text` elements in the template. Well, sort of—because the `XmlDocument` object's implementation of `GetElementById` doesn't work, I have to use the `GetElementsByTagName` method to get an array containing all of the text elements in the XML:

```
. . .
XmlNodeList textNodes = tileXml.GetElementsByTagName("text");
. . .
```

The `text` nodes are returned in the order they are defined in the XML fragment, which means that I can iterate through them and set the `innerText` property of each element to one of my grocery list items:

```
...
for (int i = 0; i < textNodes.Length
    && i < viewModel.GroceryList.Count; i++) {
    textNodes[i].InnerText = viewModel.GroceryList[i].Name;
}
...
```

■ **Tip**   Only three of the four text elements defined by the XML template will be visible by the user on the Start screen. The last element is obscured by the app name or icon. This is true for many of the tile templates.

Applying the Tile Update

Once I have set the content of the XML document, I use it to create the update for the app tile. I need to create a `TileNotification` object from the XML and then pass this to the `Update` method of the `TileUpdater` object that is returned from the static `TileUpdateManager.CreateTileUpdaterForApplication` method:

```
...
for (int i = 0; i < 5; i++) {
    TileUpdateManager.CreateTileUpdaterForApplication()
        .Update(new TileNotification(tileXml));
}
...
```

Not all tile updates are processed properly in Windows 8, which is why I repeat the notification using a `for` loop. Five seems to be the smallest number of repetitions that guarantees that an update will be displayed on the Start screen.

Calling the Tile Update Method

I call my `UpdateTile` method in two situations. The first is directly from the constructor, which ensures that the tile reflects the current data in the view model when the app is started. The second situation is when the contents of the collection are changed:

```
...
viewModel.GroceryList.CollectionChanged += (sender, args) => {
    UpdateTile();
};
...
```

The `CollectionChanged` event is fired when an item is added, replaced, or removed from the collection of grocery list items. It *won't* be fired when the properties of an individual `GroceryList` object are modified. To arrange this, I'd have to add handlers to each object in the collection. There are no app-specific techniques to show you how to this, so I'll just focus on tile changes in this chapter.

Testing the Tile Update

A couple of preparatory steps are required before I can test my updating tile. First, the Visual Studio simulator doesn't support updating tiles, which means I am going to test directly on my development machine. To do this, I need to change the Visual Studio deployment target to Local Machine, as shown in Figure 4-5.

Figure 4-5. *Selecting the local machine for debugging*

The second step is to uninstall my example app from the Start screen (which you do by selecting Uninstall from the AppBar). There seems to be some "stickiness" where apps that have previously relied on static tiles don't process updates correctly.

With both of these steps completed, I can now start my app from Visual Studio by selecting Start Debugging from the Debug menu. When the app has started, I can make changes to the grocery list, and a pithy summary of the first three items will be shown on the start tile, as shown in Figure 4-6.

Figure 4-6. *Updating an app tile*

It can be difficult to get the updating tile to appear initially. Here are some of the things that I have found can help:

- Closing the simulator

- Restarting Visual Studio

- Uninstalling another (unrelated) app from the Start screen

- Searching for the GrocerApp app using the Start screen

- Moving some other tiles around the Start screen

- Restarting

It can be frustrating to get the tile to appear initially, but once it is there, everything will work as expected, and further updates to the app rarely make the tile disappear again. These problems don't happen when users install apps from the Windows Store; it is just the change from static to live files that causes the problem.

Updating Wide Tiles

The technique I showed you in the previous section is useful if you want to be able to update the square *or* the wide tile for your app. But, unless you have very specific presentation needs for your data, you should provide updates for both square and wide tiles since you have no idea which your users will select.

To update both tile sizes, you need to combine two XML templates to create a single fragment that contains both updates. In this section, I am going to combine the TileSquareText03 and TileWideBlockAndText01 templates. The wide template has a couple of additional fields, which I will use to display the number of stores that the user has to visit to get all of the items on the grocery list. You can see what I am aiming to produce in Listing 4-11: a fragment that follows the same format as a single template but that combines two binding elements.

Listing 4-11. Composing a Single XML Fragment

```
<tile>
    <visual lang="en-US">
        <binding template="TileSquareText03">
            <text id="1">Apples</text>
            <text id="2">Hotdogs</text>
            <text id="3">Soda</text>
            <text id="4"></text>
        </binding>
        <binding template="TileWideBlockAndText01">
            <text id="1">Apples (Whole Foods)</text>
            <text id="2">Hotdogs (Costco)</text>
            <text id="3">Soda (Costco)</text>
            <text id="4"></text>
            <text id="5">2</text>
```

```
                <text id="6">Stores</text>
            </binding>
        </visual>
</tile>
```

There is no convenient API for combining templates. The approach I have taken is to use the XML handling support to populate the templates separately and then combine them at the end of the process, which you can see in Listing 4-12.

Listing 4-12. Producing a Single Update for Square and Wide Tiles

```
...
private void UpdateTile() {

    int storeCount = 0;
    List<string> storeNames = new List<string>();

    for (int i = 0; i < viewModel.GroceryList.Count; i++) {
        if (!storeNames.Contains(viewModel.GroceryList[i].Store)) {
            storeCount++;
            storeNames.Add(viewModel.GroceryList[i].Store);
        }
    }

    XmlDocument narrowTileXml = TileUpdateManager
        .GetTemplateContent(TileTemplateType.TileSquareText03);
    XmlDocument wideTileXml = TileUpdateManager
        .GetTemplateContent(TileTemplateType.TileWideBlockAndText01);

    XmlNodeList narrowTextNodes = narrowTileXml.GetElementsByTagName("text");
    XmlNodeList wideTextNodes = wideTileXml.GetElementsByTagName("text");

    for (int i = 0; i < narrowTextNodes.Length
        && i < viewModel.GroceryList.Count; i++) {

        GroceryItem item = viewModel.GroceryList[i];
        narrowTextNodes[i].InnerText = item.Name;
        wideTextNodes[i].InnerText = String.Format("{0} ({1})", item.Name,
            item.Store);
    }

    wideTextNodes[4].InnerText = storeCount.ToString();
    wideTextNodes[5].InnerText = "Stores";

    var wideBindingElement = wideTileXml.GetElementsByTagName("binding")[0];
    var importedNode = narrowTileXml.ImportNode(wideBindingElement, true);
    narrowTileXml.GetElementsByTagName("visual")[0]
        .AppendChild(importedNode);
```

```
    for (int i = 0; i < 5; i++) {
        TileUpdateManager.CreateTileUpdaterForApplication()
            .Update(new TileNotification(narrowTileXml));
    }
}
...
```

The wider format tile gives me an opportunity to present more information to the user on each line; in this case, I include information about which store an item is to be purchased from in addition to the overall number of store visits required.

Combining templates isn't a difficult process to master, but you have to take care when trying to merge the two XML fragments. I have used the template for the square tile as the basis for my combined update. When I add the binding element from the wide template, I have to first import it into the square XML document, like this:

```
var importedNode = narrowTileXml.ImportNode(wideBindingElement, true);
```

The ImportNode method creates a new copy of my wide binding element in the context of my square document. The arguments to the ImportNode method are the element I want to import and a bool value indicating whether I want child nodes to be imported as well (which, of course, I do). Once I have created this new element, I insert it into the square XML using the AppendChild element:

```
narrowTileXml.GetElementsByTagName("visual")[0].AppendChild(importedNode);
```

The result is the combined document I showed you in Listing 4-11. You can see the appearance of the wide tile size in Figure 4-7. (You can toggle between the square and wide versions by selecting the tile and using the Start screen AppBar.)

Figure 4-7. *Updating a wide tile*

Applying Badges

Windows 8 manages to pack a lot of features into tiles, including support for *badges*, which are small icon or numeric overlays for a tile. The latter fall into the tile-as-an-ad category because there are very few situations in which a numeric representation does anything other than invite the user to start the app.

■ **Tip**   Although I show tiles and badges being used together, you can apply badges directly to static tiles.

To demonstrate badges, I am going to show a simple indicator based on the number of items in the grocery list. Listing 4-13 shows the additions to the MainPage class.

Listing 4-13. Adding Support for Tile Badges

```csharp
using GrocerApp.Data;
using System;
using Windows.Data.Xml.Dom;
using Windows.UI.Notifications;
using Windows.UI.Xaml;
using Windows.UI.Xaml.Controls;
using Windows.UI.Xaml.Navigation;
using System.Collections.Generic;

namespace GrocerApp.Pages {

    public sealed partial class MainPage : Page {
        private ViewModel viewModel;

        public MainPage() {
            this.InitializeComponent();

            viewModel = new ViewModel();

            // ...test data removed for brevity...

            this.DataContext = viewModel;

            MainFrame.Navigate(typeof(ListPage), viewModel);

            viewModel.GroceryList.CollectionChanged += (sender, args) => {
                UpdateTile();
                UpdateBadge();
            };

            UpdateTile();
            UpdateBadge();
        }

        private void UpdateBadge() {

            int itemCount = viewModel.GroceryList.Count;
```

```
        BadgeTemplateType templateType = itemCount > 3
            ? BadgeTemplateType.BadgeGlyph : BadgeTemplateType.
            BadgeNumber;

        XmlDocument badgeXml = BadgeUpdateManager.GetTemplateContent(te
            mplateType);
        ((XmlElement)badgeXml.GetElementsByTagName("badge")[0]).
            SetAttribute("value",
            (itemCount > 3) ? "alert" : itemCount.ToString());

        for (int i = 0; i < 5; i++) {
            BadgeUpdateManager.CreateBadgeUpdaterForApplication()
                .Update(new BadgeNotification(badgeXml));
        }
    }

    private void UpdateTile() {
        // ...code removed for brevity...
    }

    protected override void OnNavigatedTo(NavigationEventArgs e) {
    }

    private void NavBarButtonPress(object sender, RoutedEventArgs e) {
        Boolean isListView = (Button)sender == ListViewButton;
        MainFrame.Navigate(isListView ? typeof(ListPage)
            : typeof(DetailPage), viewModel);

    }
  }
}
```

Badges work in a similar way to tile notifications. You obtain an XML template, populate the content, and use it to present some information to the user via the Start screen. Two types of badge template are available; the first, the numeric template, will display a numeric value between 1 and 99, and the second, the glyph template, will display a small image from a limited range defined by Windows.

The numeric and glyph templates are the same and, as Listing 4-14 shows, are much simpler than the ones I used for tiles.

Listing 4-14. The Template for Numeric and Image Badges

```
<badge value=""/>
```

The objective is to set the value attribute to either a numeric value or the name of a glyph. I display a numeric badge if there are three or fewer items on the grocery list. If there are more than three items, then I use an icon to indicate that the user should be concerned about the extent of their shopping obligations.

The process for creating a badge begins with selecting a template. The two template types are Windows.UI.Notifications.BadgeTemplateType; for numeric badges, you use the BadgeNumber template, and the BadgeGlyph template is used for icons. You could use the same template in both situations because they return the same XML. This may change in later releases, so it is prudent to select the right template, even though the content is the same.

The next step is to locate the value attribute in the XML and assign it either a numeric value or the name of an icon. The numeric range for badges is very specific; it is from 1 to 99. If you set the value less than 1, the badge won't be displayed at all. Any value greater than 99 results in a badge showing 99.

The list of icons is equally prescriptive. You cannot use your own icons and must choose from a list of ten that Windows supports. You can see a list of the icons at goo.gl/ YoYee. For this example, I have chosen the alert icon, which looks like an asterisk. Once the XML is populated, you create a new BadgeNotification object and use it to post the update. As with tiles, I find that not all badges updates are processed, so I repeat the update five times to make sure it gets through:

```
...
for (int i = 0; i < 5; i++) {
    BadgeUpdateManager.CreateBadgeUpdaterForApplication()
        .Update(new BadgeNotification(badgeXml));
}
...
```

All that remains is to ensure that my badge updates are created. To do this, I have changed the event handler for the grocery list events so that the tile and the badge are updated together. You can see the four different badge/tile configurations in Figure 4-8: wide and square tiles, with number and icon badges.

Figure 4-8. Displaying a badge on a tile

Summary

In this chapter, I showed you how to adapt to snapped and filled views and how to use tiles to provide your users with enticements to run your app or the data they require to avoid doing so. These features are essential in delivering an app that is integrated into the broader Windows 8 experience.

You may feel that the amount of space available in a snapped layout is too limited to offer any serious functionality, but with some careful consideration, it is possible to focus on the essence of the service that you offer and omit everything else. If all else fails, you can present an information-only summary of your app and explicitly break out of the layout.

Careful consideration is also required to get the most from tiles and badges. Well-thought-out badges can significantly improve the attractiveness or utility of your app, but ill-considered tiles are annoying or just plain useless.

CHAPTER 5

■ ■ ■

App Life Cycle and Contracts

In this, the final chapter in this book, I show you how to take control of the app life cycle by responding to key Windows events. I show you how to fix the code that Visual Studio adds to projects, how to properly deal with your app being suspended and resumed, and how to implement contracts that tie your app into the wider user experience that Windows 8 offers. Along the way, I'll demonstrate the use of the geolocation feature and show you how to set up and manage a recurring asynchronous task. Table 5-1 provides the summary for this chapter.

Table 5-1. *Chapter Summary*

Problem	Solution	Listing
Ensure that your app receives the life-cycle events.	Handle the Suspending and Resuming events defined in the Application class.	1–2
Ensure the clean termination of a background task when the app is suspended.	Request a deferral and use the five-second grace period that this provides to prepare for suspension.	3–6
Implement a contract.	Add the feature implementation in your code and override the Application method so you receive the life-cycle event when the contract is invoked.	7–9

Dealing with the App Life Cycle

In Chapter 1, I showed you the skeletal code that Visual Studio placed into the App.xaml.cs file to give me a jump start with my example project. This code handles the Windows app *life-cycle events*, ensuring that I can respond appropriately to the signals that the operating system is sending me. There are three key stages in the life of a Windows app.

The first stage, *activation*, occurs when your app is started. The Windows runtime will load and process your content and signal when everything is ready. It is during activation that I generate the dynamic content for my example app, for example.

Users don't typically close Windows apps; they just move to another app and leave the Windows to sort things out. This is why there are no close buttons or menu bars on a Windows app UI. An app that is no longer required is moved into the second stage and is *suspended*. While suspended, no execution of the app code takes place, and there is no interaction with the user.

If the user switches back to a suspended app, then the third stage occurs: the app is *restored*. The app is displayed to the user, and execution of the app resumes. Suspended apps are not always restored; if the device is low on memory, for example, Windows may simply terminate a suspended app.

Correcting the Visual Studio Event Code

The first change I need to make is to remove the view model from the MainPage.xaml. cs code-behind file. I have been moving the view model gradually to demonstrate the central role that it plays in a Windows app, and in this chapter, there are features I am going to show you that require the view model to be created as part of the life cycle. You can see the simplified MainPage.xaml.cs file in Listing 5-1.

Listing 5-1. Removing the View Model Instantiation from the MainPage.xaml.cs File

```
using GrocerApp.Data;
using System;
using Windows.Data.Xml.Dom;
using Windows.UI.Notifications;
using Windows.UI.Xaml;
using Windows.UI.Xaml.Controls;
using Windows.UI.Xaml.Navigation;

namespace GrocerApp.Pages {

    public sealed partial class MainPage : Page {
        private ViewModel viewModel;

        public MainPage() {
            this.InitializeComponent();
        }

        private void UpdateBadge() {
            // ...statements omitted for brevity...
        }

        private void UpdateTile() {
            // ...statements omitted for brevity...
        }

        protected override void OnNavigatedTo(NavigationEventArgs e) {
            viewModel = (ViewModel)e.Parameter;
            this.DataContext = viewModel;

            MainFrame.Navigate(typeof(ListPage), viewModel);
```

```
viewModel.GroceryList.CollectionChanged += (sender, args) => {
    UpdateTile();
    UpdateBadge();
};

UpdateTile();
UpdateBadge();
}

private void NavBarButtonPress(object sender, RoutedEventArgs e) {
    Boolean isListView = (Button)sender == ListViewButton;
    MainFrame.Navigate(isListView ? typeof(ListPage)
        : typeof(DetailPage), viewModel);

}
}
}
```

I can now turn to the App.xaml.cs file and build on the template code to respond to changes in the app life cycle. Unfortunately, the code for handling the life-cycle events that Visual Studio adds to a project doesn't work. It deals with activation and suspension quite happily, but it prevents the app from being notified when it is being restored. Fortunately, the solution to this is pretty simple, and you can see the changes required to App.xaml.cs in Listing 5-2.

Listing 5-2. Handling the Life-Cycle Notification Events

```
using GrocerApp.Data;
using System;
using Windows.ApplicationModel;
using Windows.ApplicationModel.Activation;
using Windows.UI.Xaml;
using Windows.UI.Xaml.Controls;

namespace GrocerApp {

    sealed partial class App : Application {
        private ViewModel viewModel;

        public App() {
            this.InitializeComponent();

            viewModel = new ViewModel();

            viewModel.StoreList.Add("Whole Foods");
            viewModel.StoreList.Add("Kroger");
            viewModel.StoreList.Add("Costco");
            viewModel.StoreList.Add("Walmart");
```

```csharp
        viewModel.GroceryList.Add(new GroceryItem {
            Name = "Apples",
            Quantity = 4, Store = "Whole Foods"
        });
        viewModel.GroceryList.Add(new GroceryItem {
            Name = "Hotdogs",
            Quantity = 12, Store = "Costco"
        });
        viewModel.GroceryList.Add(new GroceryItem {
            Name = "Soda",
            Quantity = 2, Store = "Costco"
        });
        viewModel.GroceryList.Add(new GroceryItem {
            Name = "Eggs",
            Quantity = 12, Store = "Kroger"
        });

        this.Suspending += OnSuspending;
        this.Resuming += OnResuming;
    }

    protected override void OnLaunched(LaunchActivatedEventArgs args) {
        Frame rootFrame = Window.Current.Content as Frame;

        if (rootFrame == null) {
            rootFrame = new Frame();
            if (args.PreviousExecutionState == ApplicationExecutionState.
            Terminated)
            {
                //TODO: Load state from previously suspended application
            }
            Window.Current.Content = rootFrame;
        }

        if (rootFrame.Content == null) {

            if (!rootFrame.Navigate(typeof(Pages.MainPage), viewModel)) {
                throw new Exception("Failed to create initial page");
            }
        }
        Window.Current.Activate();
    }

    private void OnResuming(object sender, object e) {
        viewModel.GroceryList[1].Name = "Resume";
    }
```

```
private void OnSuspending(object sender, SuspendingEventArgs e) {
    var deferral = e.SuspendingOperation.GetDeferral();
    viewModel.GroceryList[0].Name = "Suspend";
    deferral.Complete();
  }
 }
}
```

I have highlighted the most important change, which is to register for the Suspending and Resuming events, and added statements to the handler methods for those event. Visual Studio includes a handler for the Suspending event when it created the class, but I had to add the Resuming handler to get the event notification. I removed the code in the OnLaunched method, which tried (and failed) to work out when the app was being resumed.

My app doesn't currently perform any tasks that are affected by the app being suspended and resumed at the moment, but I want to show you how to test for the events. To that end, I respond to the Suspending and Resuming events by changing the Name property of the first two items in the GroceryList collection in the view model to signal when these events have been received.

Simulating the Life-Cycle Events

The easiest way to simulate the life-cycle events is to use Visual Studio. When you start an app with the debugger, Visual Studio displays a menu to the toolbar that allows you to send the life-cycle events to the app, which I have highlighted in Figure 5-1.

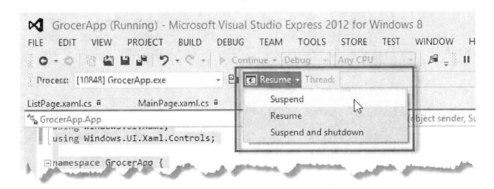

Figure 5-1. *The Visual Studio button to send life-cycle events to an app*

If you select the menu items to suspend and then resume the app, you will see the changes in the view model data shown in Figure 5-2. (You won't see the changes until you resume the app; once the app has been suspended, no UI updates are processed.)

Figure 5-2. Indicating that the life-cycle events have been receiveds

Testing the Life-Cycle Events

The problem with simulating the life-cycle events is that you don't get quite the same result as when they arise naturally. To do this, you need to start the app without the debugger, which is why indicating that the events have been received via the view model is so useful. Creating the circumstances in which the events are sent requires some specific actions, which I describe step-by-step in the following sections.

Activate the App

To trigger the `activated` event, start the app by selecting Start Without Debugging from the Visual Studio Debug menu. You can also start the app from the Start screen, either in the simulator or on your local machine. The important thing is not to start the app with the debugger.

Suspend the App

The easiest way to suspend the app is to switch to the desktop by pressing Win+D. Open the Task Manager, right-click the item for your app, and select Go to Details from the pop-up menu. The Task Manager will switch to the Details tab and select the `WWAHost.exe` process, which is responsible for running the app. After a few seconds, the value shown in the Status column will change from Running to Suspended, which tells you that Windows has suspended the app. The app will have been sent the Suspending event (but you won't see the evidence of this until the app is resumed).

Resuming the App

Switching back to the app will resume it. You will see that the view model items show that the events have been received. The state of a resumed app is exactly as it was at the moment it was suspended. Your layout, data, event handlers, and everything else will be just as it was.

Your app could have been suspended for a long time, especially if the device was put into a low-power state (such as sleeping). Network connections will have been closed by any servers you were talking to (so you should close them explicitly when you get the Suspending event) and will have to be reopened when your app is resumed. You will also have to refresh data that may have become stale; this includes location data, since the device may have been moved during the period your app was suspended.

■ **Tip** Windows allows users to terminate apps by pressing Alt+F4. There is no helpful warning event that gives you the opportunity to tidy up your data and operations. Instead, Windows just terminates your app's process.

Adding a Background Activity

Now that I have confirmed that my app can get and respond to the Resuming and Suspending events, I can add some functionality that requires a recurring background task. For this example, I am going to use the geolocation service to report on the current device location. To start, I have created a new class file called Location.cs in the Data project folder. The contents of this file are shown in Listing 5-3.

Listing 5-3. The Location.cs File

```
using System;
using System.Net.Http;
using System.Threading.Tasks;
using Windows.Data.Json;
using Windows.Devices.Geolocation;

namespace GrocerApp.Data {
    class Location {

        public static async Task<string> TrackLocation() {
            Geolocator geoloc = new Geolocator();
            Geoposition position = await geoloc.GetGeopositionAsync();

            HttpClient httpClient = new HttpClient();
            httpClient.BaseAddress = new Uri("http://nominatim.
                                    openstreetmap.org");
            HttpResponseMessage httpResult = await httpClient.GetAsync(
                String.Format("reverse?format=json&lat={0}&lon={1}",
                position.Coordinate.Latitude, position.Coordinate.
                Longitude));
```

```
        JsonObject jsonObject = JsonObject
            .Parse(await httpResult.Content.ReadAsStringAsync());

        return jsonObject.GetNamedObject("address")
            .GetNamedString("road") + DateTime.Now.ToString
            ("' ('HH:mm:ss')'");
    }
  }
}
```

This class uses the Windows 8 geolocation feature to get the location of the device. This feature is exposed through the Geolocator class in the Windows.Devices. Geolocation namespace, and the GetGeopositionAsync method gets a single snapshot of the location (as opposed to providing location updates via events, which is the other approach supported by the Geolocator class).

■ **Caution**   The new C# await keyword signals that I have entered realms of parallel/ asynchronous programming. This is an advanced example that uses the Task Parallel Library (TPL) to create and manage background tasks. I won't go into the details of TPL and .NET parallel programming in this short book. If you want more information, then I suggest my *Pro .NET 4 Parallel Programming in C#* book, which provides full details. The await keyword is a new addition to C# 4.5, which means "wait for this asynchronous task to complete."

Once I get the position of the device, I make an HTTP request to a reverse geocoding service, which allows me to translate the latitude and longitude information from the geolocation service into a street address. The geocoding service returns a JSON string, which I parse into a C# object so that I read the street information. The result from the TrackLocation method is a string listing the name of the street the device is on and a timestamp indicating the time of the location update.

■ **Tip**   I have used the OpenStreetMap geocoding service because it doesn't require a unique account token. This means you can run the example without having to create a Google Maps or Bing Maps developer account.

Extending the View Model

I am going to extend the view model so that it keeps track of the location data generated by the TrackLocation method. This will allow me to use data binding to display the data to the user. Listing 5-4 shows the additions I have made to the ViewModel class.

Listing 5-4. Updating the View Model to Capture the Location Data

```
using System.Collections.Generic;
using System.Collections.ObjectModel;
using System.ComponentModel;

namespace GrocerApp.Data {
    public class ViewModel : INotifyPropertyChanged {
        private ObservableCollection<GroceryItem> groceryList;
        private List<string> storeList;
        private int selectedItemIndex;
        private string homeZipCode;
        private string location;

        public ViewModel() {
            groceryList = new ObservableCollection<GroceryItem>();
            storeList = new List<string>();
            selectedItemIndex = -1;
            homeZipCode = "NY 10118";
            location = "Unknown";
        }

        public string Location {
            get { return location; }
            set { location = value; NotifyPropertyChanged("Location"); }
        }

        // ...other properties removed for brevity...

        public event PropertyChangedEventHandler PropertyChanged;
        private void NotifyPropertyChanged(string propName) {
            if (PropertyChanged != null) {
                PropertyChanged(this, new PropertyChangedEventArgs(propName));
            }
        }
    }
}
```

Displaying the Location Data

I have updated the MainPage.xaml file to add controls that will display the location data to the user. The data binding ensures that the current information from the view model is used, which means that no changes are required to the code-behind file. Listing 5-5 shows the additional controls.

Listing 5-5. Adding Controls to the XAML File to Display the Location Data

```xaml
<Page
    x:Class="GrocerApp.Pages.MainPage"
    xmlns="http://schemas.microsoft.com/winfx/2006/xaml/presentation"
    xmlns:x="http://schemas.microsoft.com/winfx/2006/xaml"
    xmlns:local="using:GrocerApp.Pages"
    xmlns:d="http://schemas.microsoft.com/expression/blend/2008"
    xmlns:mc="http://schemas.openxmlformats.org/markup-compatibility/2006"
    mc:Ignorable="d">

    <Page.TopAppBar>
        <AppBar>
            <StackPanel Orientation="Horizontal" HorizontalAlignment="Center">
                <Button x:Name="ListViewButton"
                    Style="{StaticResource AppBarButtonStyle}"
                    AutomationProperties.Name="List View"
                    Content="&#xE14C;" Click="NavBarButtonPress"/>

                <Button x:Name="DetailViewButton"
                    Style="{StaticResource AppBarButtonStyle}"
                    AutomationProperties.Name="Detail View"
                    Content="&#xE1A3;" Click="NavBarButtonPress"/>
            </StackPanel>
        </AppBar>
    </Page.TopAppBar>

    <Grid Background="{StaticResource AppBackgroundColor}">
        <Grid.RowDefinitions>
            <RowDefinition Height="Auto"/>
            <RowDefinition Height="*"/>
        </Grid.RowDefinitions>

        <StackPanel Orientation="Horizontal" HorizontalAlignment="Center" >
            <TextBlock FontSize="30" Text="Your location is:" Margin="0,0,10,0" />
            <TextBlock FontSize="30" Text="{Binding Path=Location}" />
        </StackPanel>

        <Frame x:Name="MainFrame" Grid.Row="1"/>
    </Grid>
</Page>
```

Declaring the App Capabilities

Apps must declare their need to access the location service in their manifest. Before running the updated app, open `package.appxmanifest`, switch to the Capabilities tab, ensure that the Location capability is checked (as shown in Figure 5-3), and save the file.

Your app will also need the Internet (Client) capability, but this is declared by default when Visual Studio creates the project.

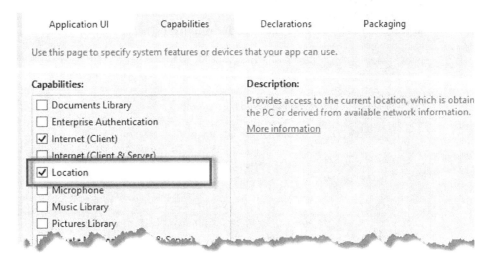

Figure 5-3. *Enabling capabilities in the manifest*

Controlling the Background Task

With all the plumbing in place, I can turn to the management of the background task and the integration with the life-cycle events, which are, after all, the point of this example. Listing 5-6 shows the changes I have made to the App.xaml.cs file.

■ **Caution** Once again, this is an advanced example. If you are not familiar with the .NET model for parallel programming, then skip to the next section where I demonstrate how to implement Windows contracts in your app.

Listing 5-6. Updating the App.xaml.cs File for the Background Task

```
using GrocerApp.Data;
using System;
using System.Threading;
using System.Threading.Tasks;
using Windows.ApplicationModel;
using Windows.ApplicationModel.Activation;
using Windows.UI.Core;
using Windows.UI.Xaml;
using Windows.UI.Xaml.Controls;
```

```
namespace GrocerApp {

    sealed partial class App : Application {
        private ViewModel viewModel;
        private Task locationTask;
        private CancellationTokenSource locationTokenSource;

        public App() {
            this.InitializeComponent();

            viewModel = new ViewModel();

            // ...test data removed for brevity...

            this.Suspending += OnSuspending;
            this.Resuming += OnResuming;
        }

        protected override void OnLaunched(LaunchActivatedEventArgs args) {
            Frame rootFrame = Window.Current.Content as Frame;

            if (rootFrame == null) {
                rootFrame = new Frame();
                Window.Current.Content = rootFrame;
            }

            if (rootFrame.Content == null) {

                if (!rootFrame.Navigate(typeof(Pages.MainPage), viewModel)) {
                    throw new Exception("Failed to create initial page");
                }
            }
            Window.Current.Activate();
            StartLocationTracking(rootFrame);
        }

        private void OnResuming(object sender, object e) {
            viewModel.Location = "Unknown";
            StartLocationTracking(Window.Current.Content as Frame);
        }

        private void OnSuspending(object sender, SuspendingEventArgs e) {
            StopLocationTracking();
            SuspendingDeferral deferral = e.SuspendingOperation.GetDeferral();
```

```
            locationTask.Wait();
            deferral.Complete();
        }

        private void StartLocationTracking(Frame frame) {
            locationTokenSource = new CancellationTokenSource();
            CancellationToken token = locationTokenSource.Token;

            locationTask = new Task(async () => {
                while (!token.IsCancellationRequested) {
                    await frame.Dispatcher.RunAsync(CoreDispatcherPriority.
                    Normal,
                        async () => {
                            viewModel.Location = await Location.
                            TrackLocation();
                        });
                    token.WaitHandle.WaitOne(5000);
                }
            });
            locationTask.Start();
        }

        private void StopLocationTracking() {
            locationTokenSource.Cancel();
        }
    }
}
```

The changes to this class represent two different activities. The first is to track the location of the user as a background task and is contained in the StartLocationTracking and StopLocationTracking methods. I want you to treat these methods as black boxes because I can't explore the TPL concepts and features I rely on. The important information is that the StartLocationTracking method starts a background activity that reports on the location every five seconds, and the StopLocationTracking method cancels that task.

What I *do* want to talk about is how I integrate this background task with the life-cycle events. Responding when the app is started or in response to the Resuming event is easy; I simply call the StartLocationTracking method.

For the Suspending event, I want to make sure that my background task has completed before the app is suspended. If I don't take this step, then I run the risk of either displaying stale data when the app is resumed or causing an error by trying to read from a network request that has been closed by the server during the period that my app was suspended.

To help work around this problem, the SuspendingEventArgs. SuspendingOperation.GetDeferral method tells the Windows runtime that I am not quite ready for my app to be suspended and that I need a little more time. This gives me a short window in which to wait for my task to complete. The GetDeferral method returns a SuspendingDeferral object, and I call its Complete method when I am ready for my app to be suspended.

Asking for a deferral grants an extra five seconds to prepare for suspension. This may not sound like a lot, but it is pretty generous given that Window may be under a lot of pressure to get your app out of the way to make system resources available.

Dispatching the UI Update

One other aspect of Listing 5-6 that is worth noting is this:

```
...
await frame.Dispatcher.RunAsync(CoreDispatcherPriority.Normal,
    async () => {
        viewModel.Location = await Location.TrackLocation();
});
...
```

Windows will allow updates to UI controls to be made only from a designated thread; this is the thread that was used to instantiate my app. If I update my view model from my background task, the events that are emitted because of the update ultimately result in the wrong thread attempting to update the data binding and display the location to the user. This results in an exception that will be reported with this kind of detailed message:

```
The application called an interface that was marshalled for a different
thread
```

I need to make sure that I use a `Dispatcher` to push my updates on the correct thread. However, there isn't a `Dispatcher` available within the `Application` class that my App class is derived from. To solve this problem, I use the `Dispatcher` from the `Frame` control that is created in the `OnLaunched` method.

Testing the Background Task

All that remains is to test that the background task is meshing properly with the life-cycle events. The easiest way to do this is with the simulator, which supports simulated location data.

Start by defining a location in the simulator (one of the buttons on the right side of the simulator window opens the Set Location dialog box into which you can enter a location).

Once you have specified a location, start the app, remembering to do so without using the debugger. After a few seconds, you will see the location information displayed at the top of the app window, as shown in Figure 5-4.

■ **Tip**   I have used the coordinates of the Empire State Building for this example. If you want to do the same, then use the Set Location dialog to specify a latitude value of 40.748 and a longitude of -73.98.

Figure 5-4. *Displaying the location information to the user*

Switch to the desktop and use the Task Manager to monitor the app until it is suspended. While the app is suspended, use the simulator's Set Location dialog to change the location.

Resume the example app. The Resuming event will restart the background task, ensuring that fresh data is displayed.

■ **Tip** You may have to grant permission for the simulator and the app to access your location data. There is an automated process that checks the required settings and prompts you to make the required changes to your system configuration.

Implementing a Contract

Suspending and Resuming are not the only life-cycle events. There are others, and they are used by Windows as part of the system of *contracts*, which allow you app to get tighter integration with the rest of the operating system. In this section, I will demonstrate the *search* contract, which tells Windows that my app is willing and able to use the platform-wide search features.

Declaring Support for the Contract

The first step toward implementing a contract is to update the manifest. Open the Package.appxmanifest file and switch to the Declarations tab. If you open the Available Declarations menu, you will see the lists of contracts that you can declare support for. Select Search and click the Add button. The Search contract will appear on the Supported Declarations list, as shown in Figure 5-5.

Application UI	Capabilities	Declarations	Packaging

Use this page to add declarations and specify their properties.

Available Declarations:

Select one... ▼ [Add]

Description:

Registers the app as a search provider. End users are able to search the app from anywhere in Only one instance of this declaration is allowed per app.

More information

Supported Declarations:

Search [Remove]

Properties:

App settings

Executable:

Figure 5-5. *Declaring support for the search contract*

Ignore the `Properties` section for the contract; these allow you to delegate your obligations under the search contract to another app, which I won't be doing.

Implementing the Search Feature

The purpose of the search contract is to connect the operating system search system with some kind of search capability within your app. For my example app, I am going to handle search requests by iterating through the items on the grocery list and selecting the first one that contains the string the user is looking for. This won't be the most sophisticated search implementation, but it will let me focus on the contract without getting bogged down in creating lots of new code to handle searches. I have added a method to the `ViewModel` class called `SearchAndSelect`, as Listing 5-7 illustrates.

Listing 5-7. Adding Search Support to the View Model

```
using System.Collections.Generic;
using System.Collections.ObjectModel;
using System.ComponentModel;

namespace GrocerApp.Data {
    public class ViewModel : INotifyPropertyChanged {
        private ObservableCollection<GroceryItem> groceryList;
        private List<string> storeList;
        private int selectedItemIndex;
        private string homeZipCode;
        private string location;

        public ViewModel() {
            groceryList = new ObservableCollection<GroceryItem>();
            storeList = new List<string>();
            selectedItemIndex = -1;
            homeZipCode = "NY 10118";
            location = "Unknown";
        }

        public void SearchAndSelect(string searchTerm) {
            int selIndex = -1;
            for (int i = 0; i < GroceryList.Count; i++) {
                if (GroceryList[i].Name.ToLower().Contains(searchTerm.
                ToLower())) {
                    selIndex = i;
                    break;
                }
            }
            SelectedItemIndex = selIndex;
        }
```

```
// ...properties removed for brevity...

public event PropertyChangedEventHandler PropertyChanged;
private void NotifyPropertyChanged(string propName) {
    if (PropertyChanged != null) {
        PropertyChanged(this, new PropertyChangedEventArgs(propName));
    }
}
    }
}
}
```

This method will be passed the string that the user is searching for. It looks for items in the grocery list and sets the selection to the first matching item it finds or to -1 if there is no match. Since the SelectedItemIndex property is observable, this means that searching for an item will select it and display its details in the app layout.

I want the ListView control in the ListPage to select the matching item, so I have made a minor change to the ListPage.xaml.cs code-behind class, as shown in Listing 5-8.

Listing 5-8. Ensuring That the Selection Is Properly Displayed

```
...
protected override void OnNavigatedTo(NavigationEventArgs e) {

    viewModel = (ViewModel)e.Parameter;

    ItemDetailFrame.Navigate(typeof(NoItemSelected));
    viewModel.PropertyChanged += (sender, args) => {
        if (args.PropertyName == "SelectedItemIndex") {
            groceryList.SelectedIndex = viewModel.SelectedItemIndex;
            if (viewModel.SelectedItemIndex == -1) {
                ItemDetailFrame.Navigate(typeof(NoItemSelected));
                AppBarDoneButton.IsEnabled = false;
            } else {
                ItemDetailFrame.Navigate(typeof(ItemDetail), viewModel);
                AppBarDoneButton.IsEnabled = true;
            }
        }
    };
}
...
```

Responding to the Search Life-Cycle Event

The Application class makes it very easy to implement contracts by providing methods you can override for each of them. Listing 5-9 shows my implementation of the OnSearchActivated method, which is the one called when the user targets my app with a search.

Listing 5-9. Responding to Searches

```
using GrocerApp.Data;
using System;
using System.Threading;
using System.Threading.Tasks;
using Windows.ApplicationModel;
using Windows.ApplicationModel.Activation;
using Windows.UI.Core;
using Windows.UI.Xaml;
using Windows.UI.Xaml.Controls;

namespace GrocerApp {

    sealed partial class App : Application {
        private ViewModel viewModel;
        private Task locationTask;
        private CancellationTokenSource locationTokenSource;

        public App() {
            this.InitializeComponent();

            viewModel = new ViewModel();

            // ...test data omitted for brevity...
            this.Suspending += OnSuspending;
            this.Resuming += OnResuming;
        }

        protected override void OnLaunched(LaunchActivatedEventArgs args) {
            Frame rootFrame = Window.Current.Content as Frame;

            if (rootFrame == null) {
                rootFrame = new Frame();
                Window.Current.Content = rootFrame;
            }

            if (rootFrame.Content == null) {

                if (!rootFrame.Navigate(typeof(Pages.MainPage), viewModel)) {
                    throw new Exception("Failed to create initial page");
                }
            }
            Window.Current.Activate();
            StartLocationTracking(rootFrame);
        }
```

```
protected override void OnSearchActivated(SearchActivatedEventArgs args) {
    viewModel.SearchAndSelect(args.QueryText);
}

private void OnResuming(object sender, object e) {
    // ...statements omitted for brevity...
}

private void OnSuspending(object sender, SuspendingEventArgs e) {
    // ...statements omitted for brevity...
}

private void StartLocationTracking(Frame frame) {
    // ...statements omitted for brevity...
}

private void StopLocationTracking() {
    locationTokenSource.Cancel();
}
    }
}
```

That is all that is required to satisfy the obligations of the search contract; by overriding the OnSearchActivated method, I have added the ability for Windows to search my app on behalf of the user.

Testing the Search Contract

To test the contract, start the example app. It doesn't matter if you start it with or without the debugger. Bring up the charms bar and select the search icon. The example app will be selected as the target of the search automatically. To begin a search, just start typing.

When you press the search button to the right of the textbox, Windows will invoke the search contract and pass the query string to the example app. You want to search for something that will make a match, so type **hot** (so that your search will match against the hot dogs item in the grocery list) and click the button. You will see something similar to Figure 5-6.

Figure 5-6. Searching the app with a contract

I really like the contract approach. This is a very simple implementation of the search contract, but you can see how easy it is to integrate into Windows with just a few lines of code. You can go well beyond what I have done here and completely customize the way that your app deals with and responds to search.

Summary

In this chapter, I have shown you how to use the life-cycle events to respond to the way in which Windows manages apps. I described the key events and showed you how to respond to them to ensure that you app is receiving and processing them correctly.

Particular care must be taken to cleanly wrap up background tasks when an app is being suspended, and I showed you how to get control of this process by requesting a suspension deferral, allowing an extra few seconds to minimize the risk of potential errors or stale data when the app is resumed.

Finally, I showed you how life-cycle events allow you to fulfill the contracts that bind an app to the wider Windows platform and how easy it is to meet the obligations those contracts specify. I showed you the search contract, but there are several others, and I recommend you take the time to explore them fully. The more contracts you implement, the more integrated your app becomes with the rest of Windows and with other integrated apps.

In this book, I set out to show you the core system features that will jump start your app development. I have shown you how to use data bindings, how to use the major structural controls, how to deal with snapped and filled layouts, how to customize your app's tile, and, in this chapter, how to take control of the app life cycle. With these skills as your foundation, you will be able to create rich and expressive apps and get a head start on Windows 8 development. I wish you every success in your app development projects.

Index

CPSIA information can be obtained at www.ICGtesting.com
Printed in the USA
LVOW080130211212

312722LV00016B/971/P